Season

BIG FLAVORS, BEAUTIFUL FOOD

RECIPES & PHOTOGRAPHS BY

Nik Sharma

CHRONICLE BOOKS

SAN FRANCISCO

Library of Congress Cataloging-in-Publication Data

Names: Sharma, Nik, author.
Title: Season / by Nik Sharma ; photographs/
    illustrations by Nik Sharma.
Description: San Francisco : Chronicle Books, 2018. |
    Includes index.
Identifiers: LCCN 2017051015 | ISBN 9781452163994
    (hardcover : alk. paper)
Subjects: LCSH: Cooking (Spices) | Spices—India. |
    Cooking, Indic. | LCGFT: Cookbooks.
Classification: LCC TX819.A1 S525 2018 |
    DDC 641.6/383—dc23 LC record available at
    https://lccn.loc.gov/2017051015

Manufactured in China.

Prop styling by Nik Sharma
Food styling by Nik Sharma
Designed by Alice Chau

10 9 8 7 6 5 4 3 2 1

Chronicle books and gifts are available at special quantity
discounts to corporations, professional associations, literacy pro-
grams, and other organizations. For details and discount informa-
tion, please contact our premiums department at corporatesales@
chroniclebooks.com or at 1-800-759-0190.

Chronicle Books LLC
680 Second Street
San Francisco, California 94107
www.chroniclebooks.com

To my parents and my husband, Michael.
To my readers of A Brown Table *and*
A Brown Kitchen.

FOREWORD

Was it Twitter? Facebook? I don't remember the portal that drew me into Nik Sharma's blog back in 2015, before I knew anything about him, but I recall feeling the tug of having clicked into something revolutionary.

There was nothing overtly challenging about scrolling through Nik's blog, *A Brown Table*. In a way, his process shots of pastry-making were anything but iconoclastic. They showed softly blistered yeast doughs, book-fold sheets of yellow puff paste, cooked fruit bubbling through vents in crusts, against backdrops that receded into blackness, as in seventeenth-century Italian still lifes. Just like the ones in Giuseppe Recco's paintings of fruit or flowers, the inanimate objects in Nik's pictures were luminous.

It was his hands in the photos that made me stop.

Pressed on a rolling pin or clapping to clean themselves and launching a nimbus of flour, Nik's hands—brown fingers and creased palms—were unlike anything I'd seen in conventional food media. In a space remarkable for near-exclusive whiteness, Nik's posts were subversive, pushing against the visual rules of food.

They challenged biased assumptions about who *belongs* in food, about who *owns* blueberry pie and kouign amann, about who gets to cook French food and who has to be labeled as "ethnic."

It was only later, when I learned to look beyond the pictures, that I realized the vocabulary of Nik's new language was more than merely visual. You hold the evidence in your hands, in this book. Recipes for Curry Leaf Popcorn Chicken, Butternut Squash and Tea Soup, Crab Cakes with Lemongrass and Green Mango—they tell familiar stories, with a fresh voice. The same is true of Nik's Indian recipes, dishes such as Tandoori Swordfish Steaks and Lamb Chops with Red Lentils, things that carry the weight of tradition in new ways, wrapped in new narratives, refusing to be pushed into old boxes.

In *Season*, just as at *A Brown Table*, Nik Sharma shows us a world we've never quite seen before, and begins patiently to teach us its language of vivid and sometimes unexpected flavors. With deft hands he invites us to his table: a place where everyone belongs.

JOHN BIRDSALL

CONTENTS

INTRODUCTION 10

FLAVOR GLOSSARY 23

CHAPTER 1: Small Bites 31

Grilled Dates and Raisins with
  Black Pepper and Honey 33

Chipotle–Garam Masala Olives 34

Chile-Sumac-Pomegranate Nuts 37

Chickpea-Battered Fried Okra 38

Sweet Potato Fries with Basil Yogurt Sauce 40

Broiled Herbed Oysters 42

Smoked Sardines and Kumquat Crostini 47

Curry Leaf Popcorn Chicken 48

Spiced Beef Kebabs 52

Crispy Pork Belly Bites 54

CHAPTER 2: Salads + Soups 57

Toasted Cumin and Lime Cucumber Salad 59

Caprese Salad with Sweet Tamarind Dressing 60

Rainbow Root Raita 63

Roasted Cauliflower, Paneer, and Mixed Lentil Salad 64

Chouriço Potato Salad 69

Butternut Squash and Tea Soup 70

Cocoa-Spiced Bean and Lentil Soup 73

Toasted Naan and Chicken Soup 76

Chicken Noodle Soup with Omani Limes 79

Bone and Lentil Broth 80

THE WHYS OF SEASONING 82

CHAPTER 3: Grains + Vegetables 89

Granola Two Ways 91

Naan 94

Margherita Naan Pizza 99

Ginger-Lentil Millet Bowl 100

Eggplant Pilaf 102

Shaved Brussels Sprouts with Poppy Seeds,
  Black Mustard, and Coconut Oil 105

Charred Snap Peas and Fennel with
  Bacon-Guajillo Salt 106

Roasted Young Carrots with
  Sesame, Chili, and Nori 109

Fingerlings with Crispy Sage and
  Garlicky Kefir Crème Fraîche 110

CHAPTER 4: Seafood 113

Oysters with Passion Fruit Mignonette 115

Turmeric and Lime Mussel Broth 116

Sumac-Seared Scallops with Mostarda 119

Grilled Grape Leaf–Wrapped Shrimp 120

Crab Cakes with Lemongrass and Green Mango 123

Ginger-Garlic Stir-Fried Crab 124

Tandoori Swordfish Steaks 127

Turmeric-and-Chile-Roasted
  Red Snapper with Melon Salsa 130

Coriander Gravlax 133

CHAPTER 5: Eggs + Poultry 135

Bombay Frittata 137

Baked Eggs with Artichoke Hearts 140

Egg Salad with Toasted Coriander 143

Deviled Eggs with Creamy Tahini and Za'atar 144

Hot Green Chutney–Roasted Chicken 147

Crème Fraîche Chicken Salad 148

Turkey Leg Roast with Mixed Citrus and Juniper 151

Turkey with Cherry-Fennel Barbecue Sauce 152

Turkey-Mushroom Hand Pies 155

THE HOWS OF SEASONING 158

CHAPTER 6: **Meat** 165

Spiced Meat Loaf 167

Beef Stew with Verjus 170

Steak with Orange Peel and Coriander 173

Ground Lamb and Potato "Chops"
    with Sambal Oelek 175

Lamb Chops with Red Lentils 178

Roast Leg of Lamb 181

Chaat Masala–Grilled Pork Chops 184

Pulled Pork Tacos with Apple and Serrano Slaw 186

Homemade Goan-Style Chouriço 191

CHAPTER 7: **Sweets** 192

Watermelon-Elderflower Granita 195

Raspberry-Shiso Sorbet 196

Jaggery Ice Cream 199

Spiced Maple–Broiled Peaches 200

Spicy Chocolate Chip–Hazelnut Cookies 203

Sweet Potato Bebinca 204

Apple Masala Chai Cake 207

Date and Tamarind Loaf 210

Elderflower and Ghee Cake 215

Upside-Down Orange and Fennel Cornmeal Cake 216

Rum-Soaked Raisin Caramel Cake 220

CHAPTER 8: **Sips** 223

Lemonade Two Ways 225

Ginger and Tamarind Refresher 228

Rhubarb, Cardamom, and Rose Water Sharbat 231

Salted Tarragon Lassi 232

Saffron and Cardamom Milk 235

Spiced Mango Milkshake 236

Cardamom Iced Coffee with Coconut Milk 239

Bellini with Cardamom and Peppercorns 240

Pineapple Serrano Gin 243

Pomegranate Moscow Mule 244

Caramelized Fig and Bourbon Iced Chai 247

CHAPTER 9: **Staples** 249

Tamarind 251

Jaggery 253

Eggs (Hard-Boiled Eggs, Crispy Fried
    Eggs in Ghee) 255

Rice (Plain Rice, Simple Pilaf) 256

Garlic (Roasted Garlic, Roasted Garlic in
    Sesame Oil) 259

Dairy (Paneer, Kefir Crème Fraîche) 260

Spice Blends (Garam Masala, Chaat Masala,
    My Za'atar Blend, Chai Masala, Masala Chai) 263

Salt Blends (Curry and Makrut Lime Leaf Salt,
    Bacon-Guajillo Salt, Nori and Yuzu Ponzu Salt) 267

Fats (Ghee, My Nit'r Qibe, Spiced Sweet
    Honey Butter) 268

Pickles (Pickled Green Tomatoes with Peppercorns,
    Pickled Carrot with Fennel, Red Onions
    with Coriander, Ginger-Lemon Relish,
    Spiced Lemon Pickle) 273

Condiments and Sauces (Charred Green Garlic and
    Yuzu Ponzu Sauce, Hot Green Chutney, Sweet
    and Smoky Tahini Sauce, Cilantro Oil Dressing,
    Spicy Rhubarb Confit, Apple and Pear Mostarda,
    Blackberry Long Pepper Jam, Green Mango
    Tartar Sauce) 277

RESOURCES 282

ACKNOWLEDGMENTS 283

INDEX 285

The world is getting smaller; the advent of new technologies has changed and shaped the way we interact and think. The Internet lets us explore new cultures and countries in ways we never thought would be possible. Migrant communities have brought their cultures to our doorsteps, and the foods they've shared with us have become powerful tools of education and social justice.

Today both home cooks and chefs have a new global palette of ingredients and spices to play with. We now mention cardamom in the same breath with vanilla, and ghee is a common staple on the shelves of many grocery stores. Mango lassi? Well, it needs no introduction. Our interconnected world has transformed how we think about food, and changed the way we eat.

I am an immigrant and I tell my story through food. *Season* is a collection of my experiences and tastes. But this book is more than just a book of recipes. Here you will find my approach to cooking. When I cook, my thought process is influenced not only by my childhood in India, but also by how I was shaped by my experiences while I acclimated to my adopted new home in America using food as a tool to communicate.

This is not a traditional Indian cookbook (though I've included a few of my favorite recipes). Instead, consider it a guide to bringing new flavors from different culinary traditions into your own kitchen, and making them work for you.

I take pride in incorporating flavors, techniques, and ingredients in new and exciting ways. This, my first book, celebrates diverse cultural influences and, I hope, helps to erase labels like "ethnic" and "exotic" in the West by shedding more light on some of these ingredients. *Season* is a collection of flavors from my two worlds—India and America.

India

My story begins in India. I was born on the west coast, in Bombay. (To me it will always be Bombay, even though the name has changed to Mumbai.) Like many large, cosmopolitan cities, Bombay is a melting pot of cultures. As early as the fourth century BCE, India was a part of the ancient Silk Road, through which spices and other luxury goods were transported. Later, in the fifteenth century, Bombay became a major port for trade. The influx of traders and immigrants brought—and bring, to this day—their own cultures and habits. As a financial engine, Bombay also draws millions of Indians who come in search of work and success. The result? Bombay's cuisine is one of the most varied and cosmopolitan in the world.

Our home was diverse, too. My mom is a Roman Catholic whose family hails from the former Portuguese colony of Goa. My dad is Hindu, from the northern part of the country from a state called Uttar Pradesh. Every year we celebrated both Catholic and Hindu holidays, so my sister and I tasted an amalgamation of cultures through food. The dining table was a mosaic of Portuguese-influenced dishes from Goa overlaid with the traditional staples of north Indian cooking. From a young age, this mishmash of food influences taught me that flavor and technique are highly adaptable tools that we can use to creatively explore our world.

In most Indian households, spices and other aromatics are treasured and revered. This was true for us, too. In my dad's family, spices such as cardamom and saffron were mixed into the sweets offered to deities at *pujas* (Hindu prayer ceremonies). And limes and chile peppers were tied together in a bundle and hung outside the door to ward off bad spirits. My mother would give me a tablespoonful of freshly ground black pepper with honey to fend off colds; the combination of the spicy pepper and soothing honey always worked and still does (my nostalgic association is why I love to add pepper to sweets like the grilled dates and raisins with honey on page 33 and blackberry jam on page 281).

Much of what I learned about Indian and Western cooking came from spending time with my maternal grandmother and my parents in their kitchens. My grandmother would make her weekly stock using bones and kitchen scraps and toss in whole spices. But when she prepared her glorious meat curries, she would always grind the spices down, along with freshly grated coconut and onions, to make a thick paste. It all depends, she used to say, on what you want to create.

My parents let me cook and experiment. I pored over my mother's cookbooks and newspaper cuttings and tried baking through her collection of chocolate and Neapolitan cake recipes. My dad gave me my first whiff of raw asafetida: at the time, I thought it was the most disgusting thing I'd ever smelled. He explained that his mother avoided eating garlic and onions for religious and cultural reasons—they were considered to be aphrodisiacs. (Hopefully, this practice is dying out.) Instead, she'd add a tiny pinch of asafetida to hot oil when she cooked her food, which to my amazement had a sulfurous smell reminiscent of onion and garlic.

Cooking was a family affair. Every year, in the month leading up to the Christmas holidays, we would visit with my cousins and aunts, sitting around a long, wooden table cutting out Christmas cookies and molding cashew marzipan. These sweets would make their way to family, friends, and neighbors on Christmas Day.

I had a fairly normal childhood, but I knew I was different from a very young age. I knew I was gay. Being openly gay in India was out of the question; it was against the law, and you could be harassed, beaten, jailed, or even worse. I looked forward to more advanced academic studies because my life in high school was miserable. But I knew that if I wanted to truly be myself and feel safe, without fear of intolerance or rejection, I would have to leave the country. America was then—and still is—my first choice. In America, I could decide on the career I wanted and work hard to be successful. I could follow my dreams and my heart and take advantage of life's opportunities, regardless of who I was or where I came from. As each year passed, I continued to nurture this dream that I would eventually escape to America.

While I was studying biochemistry at the University of Bombay (Mumbai) in India, I considered graduate school in America. I thought it would open new professional opportunities for me, and I hoped it would give me the freedom to be my true self, without judgment. But my parents could not afford to pay for university. I knew I would need a scholarship. So, I studied day and night in my parents' tiny studio and took my entrance tests. I won scholarships at several universities and, eventually, decided to pursue molecular genetics at the University of Cincinnati, College of Medicine.

I remember the evening I boarded my first flight to America, when I was in my early twenties. Heavy raindrops slapped against the plane windows as I stared out into the dark monsoon sky that had enveloped Bombay. My heart beat loudly with excitement and nervous anticipation, but I was also sad, knowing this would be the last time I would see these rains and my family for a long while.

The Midwest

I arrived at the airport in Cincinnati with my life's possessions stuffed into two large pieces of luggage. Along with my clothes and shoes, I had packed a pressure cooker and some basic kitchen essentials. In India, pressure cooking is popular, and my parents insisted I'd need the appliance to cook recipes from home. But I had no intention of restricting myself to Indian cooking. I also wanted to experience as much of my new country as I could, and there was no better way to do this than through its food.

I lived in Cincinnati for four years, studying, cooking, and eating a lot of pizza. (My stipend was tiny.) I ate my first slices at local joints like Dewey's. They tasted nothing like the pizza I'd had back in India. The endless variety of toppings, the different sauces, and the variations in the crust, from thick to thin—it all delighted me.

I spent most of my time learning about genes and running experiments to understand health and disease, and in the process, I worked with people from different cultures and different parts of the world. In addition to sharing our ideas and research, we shared our food. School and lab potlucks were common and became a new source for my cultural initiation and culinary education. They inspired me to bring the food and flavors I knew to the table, and to explore the new palette of flavors and ingredients I was encountering. On some days, I would cook pasta with my mom's recipe for *kheema* (a spiced ground lamb dish) and on others, I'd make a Greek omelet with crumbled feta, spinach, and garlic and throw in a little turmeric and Garam Masala (page 263).

Within a few months of arriving in America, I decided to come out to my family and friends. The University of Cincinnati's medical school had a supportive network of LGBTQ students and professors, who were there for me from day one. But coming out to friends was much easier than coming out to my parents. I don't think my parents knew or even heard of any gay people, except for Freddie Mercury.

I sent an email first and then called my parents. I'd never felt so scared. Would they accept me, or would they cut all ties with me? My father supported me right away, but my mother had a harder time because of her strict Catholic upbringing. She had already married outside her faith, against her parents' wishes, and my coming out could jeopardize her relationship with them. But my mother loved me and accepted me, though it took her a while to come around. I was far away from the place of my birth now, but I was not alone. And I was finally free.

The East Coast

I enjoyed my research in molecular genetics in Cincinnati. Every day, I would put on my white lab coat; walk into a sterile, cold environment; and make the tiniest bit of progress on gene cloning research. I knew that my work might help improve people's lives one day, but it was starting to feel too abstract.

I decided to pack my bags and move to Washington, D.C., where I got a full-time job in the Department of Medicine at Georgetown University as a researcher for the department chair. Finally, I was running

pharmaceutical studies on very real medical conditions, such as osteoporosis, diabetes, and obesity. I could see how my work was making patients' lives better, because I was face to face with them every day. And I could watch as their health improved, thanks to our findings. At the time, I wanted to see how my research could be used to improve public health. To achieve that, I went to the Georgetown School of Public Policy, where I got a master's degree in public policy, while still working as a researcher at the Department of Medicine.

Still, something was missing. Every night, I'd come home exhausted after a full day at work and school, and I'd step into my tiny kitchen to make a quick dinner. But instead of feeling like I wanted to collapse, I became energized. My hands would itch to feel the weight of my knife cutting vegetables, or to feel the give of fresh dough under my palms.

I clearly needed a creative outlet, and so I started a fledgling online photojournal to chronicle my cooking life and explore new flavors, ingredients, and techniques. I called it *A Brown Table*. Although I lacked formal photography training and professional-grade equipment, I didn't let that deter me. Armed with a laptop and a point-and-shoot camera, I proceeded. My "studio" was a couple of wooden boards balanced atop trash cans in the kitchen of my basement condo. If others found the blog online and wanted to follow along, so be it. But that wasn't really the point early on.

Local flavors and cultures inspired me; I had a newfound appreciation for the food community. And because D.C. is the nation's capital, which attracts people from around the world, the range of international flavors was spectacular! From the vibrant Ethiopian and Eritrean community of Adams Morgan to Ben's Chili Bowl on U Street, there was a whole new dimension to food that I got to explore.

I started reinventing the dishes I was enjoying at local restaurants or at the homes of friends, often substituting or adding the familiar flavor notes of my youth. I'd season marinara with a few nigella seeds and cook chili with ground coriander and Kashmiri chile powder.

One summer, at a bar in D.C., I met Michael through a mutual friend, and we fell in love. Michael shared my passion for adventure, travel, and food, and he encouraged me to pursue my passion for cooking.

The South

Michael's family has lived in the Appalachian Mountains of Virginia for generations. They originally owned a small tobacco farm, and then, in the last century, transitioned to sugarcane. My mother-in-law, Shelly, tends a vegetable patch large enough to feed the whole extended family. She also raises goats, which she milks to make artisanal soap to sell at the farmers' market.

On my first visit to the farm to meet Michael's family, I was nervous and excited. Michael had mentioned my love of cooking to Shelly, and one night, she asked me to cook dinner for them. Because first impressions are everything, I had to make a good one. I wanted the meal to be special and new, yet familiar enough so they'd like it. Knowing they were a meat-and-potatoes family, I made a Goan specialty of stir-fried beef and hot chiles called chile fry. I served it with chicken biryani—layers of chicken, rice, and fried potatoes, cooked together.

They loved it! Because there are no Indian restaurants where they live, this was the first time they had tasted Indian food, and with all these new flavors, things could have gone very wrong. But something about the combination of new and familiar, exotic and homespun, struck the exact right note. By the end of the trip, my mother-in-law and I were standing side-by-side in the kitchen, chatting and baking cobblers and pies. Even now, whenever Michael and I visit, my mother-in-law and I cook together. And the Southern influences I've adopted from Michael and his family have given a new depth to my food.

The West Coast

I was knee-deep in learning how to make biscuits with his mom, experimenting with ghee as a replacement for the lard. We would host large meals for our friends almost every weekend during the warmer months of the year. At *A Brown Table*, I wrote less about traditional Indian food and more about the food I was creating.

Michael had lived in D.C. for more than a decade and was ready for a change from his government job. He accepted a position in San Francisco. We tied the knot and this time, packed up our bags together, and drove across the country with our dog, Snoopy, to our new home. Change begets more change. I realized I was ready to make a big career change myself. So, I quit my lucrative medical research career to pursue my dream of working in food.

My parents were not thrilled. My mother had worked in hotel management, and when I was a child, she often told me that a life peeling onions in a cold room for hours each day wasn't what she wanted for me. My dad was a commercial photographer, and though I'd grown up surrounded by cameras and professional equipment, I'd never been allowed to touch them. My parents wanted a stable and secure profession for me, and a career in food or the arts didn't fit that template.

With Michael's encouragement, I didn't waver. Instead, I asked my dad to recommend quality cameras and equipment. I pored over old photography textbooks and manuals, and considered new ways to breathe life into my photographs. I opted for risk over predictability and creativity over stability. And it has paid off. By pushing the limits of contrast, texture, and motion, I've developed a distinct visual point of view in my photographs, which has earned me awards and good press coverage.

Experimentation

By now, I was experimenting with photography as much as with food. And while I loved the freedom to follow my whimsy in both fields, I craved formal culinary training. I was considering enrolling in a school when I came across an article on the subject by David Lebovitz. Get your feet wet in a kitchen before investing time and money in school, he advised. So, I called up every local bakery and patisserie in our neighborhood, and eventually started working part time at a patisserie called Sugar Butter Flour in Sunnyvale, California. Though grueling— I began my day shift before sunrise—the fast pace was just what I needed. There were lemon tarts to assemble, cream to whip, cakes to be frosted. I was elbow deep in flour and sugar, and I could not have been happier. The pastry kitchen was full of life, a hive of frenetic activity. Here I was, surrounded by people who loved to create food as much as I did, and we lived for the messy chaos of it all.

I learned so many valuable skills and techniques during that time, and I brought them all home with me. Each day after my shift ended, I'd head home and walk straight into my kitchen to develop new recipes, write them up, and take photographs for my blog. I began photographing myself as I cooked, so my readers could imagine themselves in my shoes, bustling around in the kitchen. I had an ulterior motive as well: I wanted them to see that people who looked like me cooked and baked in kitchens all over the world. The photos represented these cooks and bakers, as well as me.

But being gay and a person of color in an online world also brought some unwanted attention and unpleasant surprises. The color of my skin touched some nerves, and I started to receive anonymous comments that made me sick to my stomach. I retreated for a while, taking a break from photographing food to think about how I wanted to proceed.

Sometimes during moments of vulnerability, you can find your strength and voice.

As I saw it, I had only two options: I could stop blogging completely or continue to do what I loved. I chose to carry on. Ultimately, the trolls' ignorance spurred me to work harder. I continued to photograph myself prepping and cooking my recipes, and I put out my best work with the hope that people would see beyond the color of my skin. Eventually, the racist comments subsided, and people began to see my work for what it was: my contribution to the new way we approach food today, playing with cultural influences and creating new dishes that speak from a deeply personal place.

A Brown Table

I'm now working on *A Brown Table*, developing, testing, writing, and shooting recipes. In 2016, I started writing my own featured food column, A Brown Kitchen, for the *San Francisco Chronicle*, where I share recipes inspired by the foods and flavors of California and India.

Mine is the story of a gay immigrant, told through food. It has been a journey of self-discovery I embarked on more than a decade ago, one that taught me to recognize the inherent tension between originality and tradition, and to opt for the former without rejecting the latter. It's been a journey of acclimatization, adaptation, and acceptance. During times of discomfort, food became my friend and teacher. It taught me to reinterpret conventional techniques and flavors and apply these reinterpretations to my food that would become a part of my new life in America. Seasoning is more than just a way to achieve flavor in the food we eat. It represents our desire to connect with our past, present, and future; it tells our story.

Hot

ALEPPO PEPPER Usually sold as ground large flakes, this pepper adds heat and brightness to food.

BLACK PEPPERCORN The whole spice that is ground to make black pepper; it's used to add heat and pungency.

CAYENNE PEPPER A bright orange-red pepper that's on the hotter end of the scale. The peppers are usually sun-dried and then ground to a powder.

CHIPOTLE CHILE A highly aromatic dried chile obtained by drying and smoking a jalapeño pepper.

CINNAMON There are two types of cinnamon available in markets: Ceylon cinnamon (top right photo, left), which is also called "true cinnamon," and cassia cinnamon (top right photo, right). They both have a warm scent and are used in both savory and sweet preparations. Ceylon cinnamon is lighter in color and less potent than cassia.

GROUND KASHMIRI CHILE + WHOLE KASHMIRI CHILE (pictured second row, fourth from left) A mild chile used to impart a bright red color to many Indian dishes, such as tandoori chicken.

GUAJILLO CHILE A milder, smokier, and slightly hotter dried chile than a chipotle.

LONG PEPPER A type of pepper that's a little hotter than black pepper, and as the name indicates, it's longer than a peppercorn.

PAPRIKA A bright red pepper sold as a finely ground powder. Hungarian paprika is sun-dried before grinding while Spanish paprika or pimentón is made by smoking the peppers with burning oak wood. They are both available in varying degrees of sweetness, and of mild to hot heat.

RAINBOW PEPPERCORNS They're all obtained from the same black peppercorn plant, but are harvested at different stages to obtain green, red, and white peppercorns (white is the mildest).

SAMBAL OELEK A hot and spicy chile paste used in Indonesian cooking.

SERRANO CHILE I use this fresh to add heat in savory foods. You can cut back on the heat by removing and discarding the ribs and the seeds.

TELLICHERRY PEPPERCORNS Black peppercorns that are allowed to grow larger in size on the vine. They lose a little heat but are much more fragrant.

THAI CHILE Much smaller than serrano chiles, but much hotter. They come in green and red varieties.

URFA BIBER CHILE FLAKES The dried flakes of a bright red chile with a smoky, chocolaty flavor used in Turkish cooking.

WHITE PEPPER White pepper is made by removing the outer skin from peppercorns and fermenting them in water for several days. This ripening and fermenting makes white pepper less hot and sharp than black pepper, with a flavor that is earthier and more complex. I don't swap these two peppercorns in recipes. Ground white pepper is often used in lighter sauces where black pepper flecks would be visually unappealing, and it's lovely in baking.

Sour

AMCHUR A fine powder with a fruity and acidic flavor, made by grinding sun-dried mangoes. It works well in barbecue sauces as well as stews and soups.

ANARDANA Sold as whole seeds or ground, anardana is made from sun-dried pomegranate arils (seedpods). It has a sweet-and-sour and slightly nutty flavor.

COCONUT VINEGAR A key ingredient in Goan cuisine, coconut vinegar is obtained through the natural fermentation of the plant's sap.

GREEN (UNRIPE) MANGO These mangoes are picked before they ripen and turn yellow on the tree. The outer skin is bright green, while the tender flesh inside is very pale yellow. In India, unripe mango is often eaten raw with a little bit of salt and crushed red pepper as a snack, but is also incorporated in dishes to add fruity and sour notes to savory foods.

OMANI LIME Also known as a "black lime," the Omani lime is a dried lime, which is often used in Persian cuisine. It has a hint of smokiness.

SUMAC A sour berry that is dried and ground to a powder. It adds acidity to savory preparations like kebabs.

TAMARIND A fruit that is sold in Asian and Mexican markets in a number of forms, including dried with the shell on (pictured second row, third from left), in blocks of pulp (pictured second row, fourth from left), or as a concentrate. I prefer the sour tamarind sold in Asian and Indian stores to the sweeter Mexican variety because it can be used in both savory and sweet preparations.

Sweeteners

BROWN SUGAR A form of sugar obtained from sugarcane juice, brown sugar contains some amount of molasses that imparts rich flavor and a deep brown color to baked goods, meat rubs, sauces—or any use you put it to.

JAGGERY An unrefined sugar, made by heating sugarcane or palm sugar juice. The result is sweetener with a pleasant mineral aftertaste with a hint of molasses. Jaggery is sold in blocks as well as ground and comes in varying shades of golden brown.

MAPLE SYRUP A thin, sweet syrup with vanilla notes obtained from the sap of sugar maple and black maple trees.

POMEGRANATE MOLASSES A sweet and tart dark liquid obtained by slowly evaporating fresh pomegranate juice.

Salts

HIMALAYAN PINK SALT A type of rock salt. It is much more flavorful than table salt, because it is rich in minerals.

KALA NAMAK Although it's referred to as black salt, it's actually a dark pinkish red because it's so rich in minerals. It releases a mild sulfurous smell (which dissipates quickly) when it comes in contact with a liquid. I usually use it in hot and sweet preparations.

FLAKY SEA SALT A salt with large crystals and a mild, salty taste. It adds texture to a finished dish.

KOSHER SALT All kosher salts are not created equal. They vary in shape and size so make sure to adjust the amount accordingly. I use the Diamond Crystal brand because the crystals dissolve very fast. Kosher salt works great in everything, especially when cooking meat.

Seeds

CARAWAY SEED A mildly peppery spice with a hint of anise used to season Indian breads.

CARDAMOM (BLACK) Although related to green cardamom, black cardamom has a bigger pod, which is dried over open flames, a process that gives it a woody, resinous aroma. I usually use it in savory dishes or add it to hot oil when seasoning stews and pilafs.

CARDAMOM (GREEN, YELLOW, AND WHITE – NOT PICTURED) White cardamom has a weaker flavor than green because it's bleached. (I usually avoid it.) Cardamom has a cooling, camphorlike flavor and is used in both sweet and savory dishes. Both the husk and the seed are edible.

CAROM SEED It looks like a small cumin seed but carries a thyme-like perfume.

CORIANDER SEED The seed of the cilantro plant. It has a smoky flavor with a hint of sweetness. Toasting enhances the earthy and woody notes of this spice.

CUMIN SEED An aromatic spice with a warm and earthy taste. It is often used in Indian cooking.

FENNEL SEED A fragrant spice with a sweet, licorice-like taste.

FENUGREEK SEED A faintly bitter spice that is usually toasted or ground into a savory spice blend.

JUNIPER BERRY Not a true berry, but a product of conifers, these have a piney perfume with a slightly peppery, citrusy taste, and are used in the making of gin and aquavit. Ground and whole, they're used to season meats, pickles, and cocktails.

MACE AND NUTMEG These two spices come from the same fruit. Mace is made from the reddish aril, or covering, and nutmeg is the seed. I usually grind or grate them as needed.

MUSTARD SEED (BLACK AND YELLOW) Don't use these interchangeably. Black mustard seeds are aromatic and pungent, while yellow mustard seeds are very mild. I use black mustard seeds for cooking and the yellow ones for pickling.

NIGELLA SEED Nigella seed has an appealing nutty flavor; it's sometimes mistakenly called onion seed. Add it to hot oil when cooking savory dishes or use it as a topping for bread or pizza.

POPPY SEED While Western cooks often use poppy seeds for their texture, in Indian cooking they're more of a seasoning agent. They can be toasted and ground and used as a paste to thicken sauces.

SESAME SEED (BLACK AND WHITE) They have a sweet and nutty taste and are also commonly used to add texture.

STAR ANISE It has a licoricelike taste that's sweeter than fennel and anise, so use it sparingly when cooking. The seeds are hidden inside the rays of the star.

VANILLA BEAN The Madagascar variety of this tropical bean is the most popular. Both the pod and the caviar—the tiny seeds—are used.

Resins and Roots

ASAFETIDA A spice with a funky smell, which, when heated in hot oil, acquires a much more pleasant scent and a pleasing flavor. It is sometimes used in Indian cooking to mimic the flavor of onions and garlic.

GARLIC Both the fresh and the ground form are highly fragrant and can add a warm taste to food.

GINGER Fresh ginger and its ground form both add warmth and a spicy aroma. They also have a bit of starch in them, which helps thicken stews.

GREEN GARLIC Although it resembles a garlic scape, green garlic is garlic that has been harvested while young, resulting in a mild taste. (A garlic scape is a stem that grows out of the maturing bulb later in the season.)

TURMERIC Like ginger, turmeric is a root. It's sold fresh, but the ground form is much more common in America. It adds a gorgeous yellow color to curries, soups, and stews.

Umami

BLACK TEA LEAVES I usually use Assam or Darjeeling tea leaves to make chai, but the leaves also add savory notes when used as a seasoning agent.

COCOA POWDER Unsweetened cocoa powder is rich in starch, and can thicken savory sauces as well as sweet ones, lending them a warm scent and an earthy flavor.

COFFEE BEAN You can use coffee beans to enhance the flavor of cocoa in desserts, or create unique umami notes.

NORI An edible seaweed that is dried and sold as sheets and used in Japanese cooking for its rich savory/umami taste. Nori is available in various kinds and colors; Yaki-nori is the most popular.

Herbs

BAY LEAF Both fresh and dried bay leaves of the bay laurel evergreen are prized for their aroma. The Indian variety of this plant has an aroma reminiscent of cinnamon.

CILANTRO Fresh cilantro leaves make an appealing garnish, but they can also be used to make flavorful herb sauces and condiments.

CURRY LEAF Sold fresh or dried, the leaves have a pleasant fragrance. I grind them into sauces and marinades or add them to hot oil to release their aroma.

MAKRUT LIME LEAF This leaf comes from the makrut lime plant, and it infuses a dish with its strong and unique citrus scent.

MINT A fragrant and cooling herb, which can be used fresh or dried in sweet and savory preparations.

TARRAGON Like most herbs, it is available fresh or dried. Fresh tarragon leaves are highly aromatic, with a cooling, licoricelike flavor.

Florals

ELDERFLOWER These highly fragrant flowers of the *Sambucus* genus are available in fresh and dried form for flavoring and medicinal purposes. They add a sweet, floral flavor to cordials, liquors, and desserts.

ORANGE BLOSSOM WATER A staple in Middle Eastern cooking, this fragrant extract is prepared by distilling the essential oils of Seville orange blossoms.

ROSE WATER Obtained by distilling the essential oils from fresh roses. It is used in many sweet and savory preparations in Middle Eastern and Indian cooking.

SAFFRON Renowned for the gorgeous orange-yellow color it imparts to food. Fortunately, a pinch of saffron strands goes a very long way, because it is one of the most expensive spices in the world.

Schools in India are highly competitive, and it's difficult to gain admission to professional schools in fields like medicine and engineering. So, my parents hired a tutor to help me with my course work for calculus and chemistry. I'd spend three evenings per week at the home of my tutor, Mrs. Ghoshal. While I was not too keen on spending so much time with my books, I always looked forward to the little snacks Mrs. Ghoshal would serve, because everything she made was delicious. Sometimes we'd eat mini samosas. Other times, she'd offer up bowls of a rich, aromatic mutton stew with a side of warm parathas (a type of Indian flatbread). It was there, through her little savory and sweet snacks, that I first learned the pleasure of beginning a meal, a conversation, or even a study session with a small bite.

I think of small bites as a way to connect with the people seated around my table. My bites offer a peek at the foods and flavors I love most. Sometimes they're a preview of what is to come. Other times they're more of a nibble, which Michael and I might serve at a gathering of family and friends with a cup of chai or a glass of wine. Whatever the occasion, I believe these little plates should be interesting and flavorful. They should play with fresh, unexpected combinations of color, aroma, taste, and texture.

For more formal dinners, when I have several courses lined up, I prefer to kick things off with lighter bites. (Otherwise I risk filling up my guests before the meal.) One of my favorite starters is thin slices of seasonal fresh fruit—guavas in spring, ripe peaches in summer—with a few thin slices of fresh Thai chile or a pinch of dried red chili flakes, and a few sprinkles of flaky Maldon salt. I'll spritz it all with fresh lemon or lime juice or garnish with a little citrus zest for a touch of brightness.

Sometimes I make bites out of leftovers. I might serve pita bread with Spiced Lemon Pickle (page 274), for example. I also like to pair simple crudités with Spiced Sweet Honey Butter (page 270) or a vibrant Hot Green Chutney (page 277).

Grilled Dates and Raisins with Black Pepper and Honey

My earliest memory of learning to cook involved this unusual method of cooking raisins. My dad would thread large raisins onto a skewer made of a dried coconut leaf and stick it directly into the flames of a gas burner for a few seconds. We'd devour the hot, blistered raisins straight off the skewer and immediately ask for more. Here's my take on this childhood favorite.

MAKES 2 TO 4 SERVINGS

---

10 Medjool dates

½ cup [70 g] raisins

¼ tsp fine sea salt

½ tsp freshly ground black pepper

2 Tbsp honey

2 cups [480 g] plain Greek yogurt (optional)

Soak three or four bamboo skewers in water for 30 minutes. Meanwhile, preheat the grill to high and brush the grill grate lightly with a little oil.

Using a paring knife, cut the dates in half lengthwise and discard the pit. Thread the dates and raisins onto separate skewers.

Place the skewers on the grill and cook, turning, until the fruits are browned in spots, about 1 minute for the raisins and up to 3 minutes for the dates.

Remove the fruit from the skewers and transfer to a serving bowl. Season the hot fruit with the salt and pepper, and toss. Drizzle with honey and serve immediately with the yogurt on the side, if desired.

THE APPROACH Dried dates and raisins are naturally rich in sugars, and because most of their moisture has been removed, they're excellent candidates for grilling. Because the fruits are so small, a few short turns on a hot grill caramelizes the sugars quickly. The resulting hint of bitterness plays well with the salt, pepper, and honey.

Chipotle–Garam Masala Olives

Briny and crunchy, breaded olives pack big flavor into small, addictive bites. These are flavored with chipotle and garam masala, an irresistible union of Western and Eastern tastes.

MAKES 6 TO 8 SERVINGS

One 12 oz [340 g] can pitted whole black olives in brine (preferably extra-large or colossal), or 2 cups [280 g] pitted brined Kalamata olives

¾ cup [105 g] all-purpose flour

2 large eggs, lightly beaten

1 cup [140 g] plain bread crumbs

1 Tbsp chopped fresh flat-leaf parsley

2 tsp dried red chili flakes

1 tsp garam masala, homemade (page 263) or store-bought

1 tsp ground chipotle chile

1 tsp fine sea salt

1 tsp freshly ground black pepper

2 cups [480 ml] neutral-tasting vegetable oil

Drain the olives in a colander and rinse under running water. Shake and transfer to a clean kitchen towel.

Put the flour and eggs in separate medium bowls. In a third medium bowl, mix the bread crumbs, parsley, chili flakes, garam masala, chipotle, salt, and pepper.

In a small heavy saucepan, preferably with high sides, heat the oil to 300°F [150°C]. Meanwhile, in batches, dredge the olives in the flour to coat, dusting off any excess. Dip in the eggs next, coating evenly, and finally, toss them in the seasoned bread crumbs.

Fry the olives in the hot oil, a few at a time, until golden brown, about 1 minute. Drain on paper towels. Serve hot.

THE APPROACH The briny taste of olives allows you to introduce other assertive flavors without overwhelming them. Here the parsley adds a fresh note while the garam masala and chipotle add a hint of warmth and smokiness without making the olives too spicy.

Chile-Sumac-Pomegranate Nuts

It's always good to have a snack on hand for unexpected guests, and even for yourself. I'm a huge fan of sweet, sour, and hot flavors, all in one bowl. So, I'll often grab different types of nuts from the freezer and season them with this fruity combination of sumac, pomegranate molasses, and cayenne. This is one of those dishes where a few ingredients tossed together produce big flavor.

MAKES 6 SERVINGS (2 CUPS [260 G])

1 Tbsp unsalted butter, melted

2 Tbsp pomegranate molasses

2 tsp jaggery or muscovado sugar

½ tsp ground anardana (see The Approach)

½ tsp ground sumac

½ tsp cayenne pepper

½ tsp fine sea salt

1 cup [140 g] raw whole cashews

½ cup [70 g] raw shelled pistachios

½ cup [60 g] raw walnut halves

Preheat the oven to 300°F [150°C]. Line a baking sheet with parchment paper and set aside.

In a medium bowl, stir together the melted butter, pomegranate molasses, jaggery, anardana, sumac, cayenne, and salt to form a smooth paste. Fold in the nuts and stir to coat evenly. Transfer to the baking sheet and spread out in a single even layer. Bake for 20 to 25 minutes, or until the nuts are a light golden brown. Remove the baking sheet from the oven and cool completely before serving. The nuts will keep in an airtight container at room temperature for up to 1 week.

THE APPROACH Anardana are dried pomegranate seeds, which are sold in both whole and ground form. Either way, it is used to add acidity in Indian cooking. Here it's combined with pomegranate molasses, ground sumac, and cayenne to give the nuts a sweet-and-sour coating with a little heat. To change things up, replace the sea salt with *kala namak* (Indian black salt).

Chickpea–Battered Fried Okra

While okra might not strike you as a likely candidate for an appetizer, it makes a great little bite when battered and fried. Choose smaller okra, which are younger and very tender. This recipe was inspired by my love for Indian pakoras, which are also made with a chickpea flour–based batter. And I've taken a cue from classic Southern fried chicken and added butter-milk to the batter for a crunchier texture and a more flavorful bite. It's best to eat these as soon as they come out of the hot oil.

MAKES 4 SERVINGS

½ cup [60 g] chickpea flour

2 tsp amchur

1 tsp ground fenugreek

1 tsp cayenne pepper

Fine sea salt

1 cup [240 ml] buttermilk

3 Tbsp water, plus more as needed

7 oz [200 g] young okra

3 cups [720 ml] neutral-tasting vegetable oil

1 lemon, quartered

In a large bowl, whisk together the chickpea flour, amchur, fenugreek, cayenne, and 1 tsp salt. Whisk in the buttermilk and water to form a slurry as thick as pancake batter. If too thick, thin with a little water. Taste and add more salt if necessary.

Rinse the okra under cold running water and gently pat dry with paper towels. Using a sharp paring knife, cut the okra in half lengthwise and fold into the chickpea batter, turning to coat evenly.

In a small heavy pot or large saucepan, heat the oil to 375°F [190°C]. Test the oil by frying one piece of battered okra, gently shaking off the excess batter before dropping it into the oil. It should bubble and quickly rise to the top. Fry for 3 to 3½ minutes, turning as needed, until golden brown. Fry the remaining okra in batches, removing them with a slotted spoon or spider. Drain on paper towels. Season with salt and serve immediately with the lemon quarters.

THE APPROACH Okra really shines when paired with acidic ingredients such as buttermilk and amchur (ground sun-dried unripe mango), especially when fried. Fenugreek adds a faint nuttiness and also aids in digestion, while the cayenne provides heat.

Sweet Potato Fries with Basil Yogurt Sauce

I love sweet potato fries, so I usually make them in large batches. Often, I'll sprinkle them with red chili flakes and a pinch of flaky sea salt for a more concentrated flavor in each bite. The creamy and fresh-tasting basil sauce makes a tasty counterpoint.

MAKES 2 SERVINGS

Basil Yogurt Sauce

¼ cup [60 g] plain full-fat Greek yogurt

1 cup [12 g] fresh basil leaves

1 bunch [85 g] scallions (white and green parts)

½ ripe avocado

1 Thai chile, seeded, if desired

1½ Tbsp fresh lime juice

4 black peppercorns

½ tsp fine sea salt

½ cup [120 ml] chilled water, plus more as needed

Sweet Potatoes

1 lb [455 g] sweet potatoes

2 Tbsp extra-virgin olive oil

1 tsp dried red chili flakes

½ tsp flaky sea salt, such as Maldon

½ tsp freshly cracked black pepper

1 Tbsp thinly sliced scallions for garnish

To make the yogurt sauce: Combine the yogurt, basil, scallions, avocado, chile, lime juice, peppercorns, salt, and water in a blender and pulse on high speed until smooth and uniform. Taste and adjust the seasoning, if necessary. You can add more water if you want the sauce a little thinner. Transfer to a serving bowl, cover with plastic wrap, and refrigerate for at least 2 hours.

To make the sweet potatoes: Preheat the oven to 425°F [220°C]. Line a baking sheet with parchment paper. Scrub the sweet potatoes under running water and pat dry. Peel and cut lengthwise into ¼ in [6 mm] thick sticks. Transfer to a medium bowl, and add the olive oil, chili flakes, salt, and pepper, and

THE APPROACH This dish features a beautiful interplay of hot and cool. The sweet potato fries are served hot straight out of the oven, and the yogurt sauce chills the palate.

toss to coat evenly. Spread out the potatoes on the prepared baking sheet and bake until lightly browned outside and soft and tender inside, 25 to 30 minutes. Remove from the oven and transfer to a serving dish.

Serve the sweet potatoes hot, and pass the yogurt sauce on the side, garnished with the sliced scallions.

Broiled Herbed Oysters

Meghana Hemphill, my best friend from grad school, grew up in New Orleans. I've spent countless vacations with her and her family, consuming copious amounts of Cajun and Creole food. It was on one of these trips that I tried my first oysters Rockefeller, which immediately became a favorite way to prepare oysters. Food-grade rock salt is available at most grocery stores and is sometimes labeled "ice-cream salt."

MAKES 4 TO 6 SERVINGS

Food-grade rock salt for roasting

24 oysters

1 cup [220 g] unsalted butter, at room temperature

¼ cup [50 g] minced shallot

⅓ cup [45 g] dry bread crumbs

½ cup [6 g] packed fresh cilantro leaves

½ cup [6 g] packed fresh mint leaves

1 serrano chile, seeded, if desired

2 tsp dried Aleppo pepper flakes

1 tsp fine sea salt

½ tsp freshly ground black pepper

¼ cup [60 ml] fresh lemon juice

½ cup [40 g] grated Parmesan

1 lemon, cut into wedges (optional)

Position a rack in the top third of the oven and preheat to 450°F [230°C]. Fill a roasting pan with rock salt to a depth of about ½ in [12 mm] and place in the oven to heat.

Meanwhile, shuck your oysters. Each oyster will have a round side and a flat side. The round side is the bottom, and the flat is the top. With the round side down and the hinge facing you, use a dish towel to secure the oyster and to protect your hand (or wear a safety glove). Wrap your hand around the oyster, and work an oyster knife into the hinge, wiggling it to and fro until you can twist it to pry the top shell from the bottom. When you feel the shell pop open, run the knife along the underside of the top shell to sever the muscle that connects to the top. Pull the top shell off and discard. Then run the knife along the underside of the oyster to sever the muscle that connects to the bottom shell. Repeat with the remaining oysters.

THE APPROACH Sautéing the shallots before they are stirred into the pulverized herbs and seasoning makes them sweeter and less pungent. Blending fresh herbs, lemon juice, and Aleppo pepper flakes with melted butter infuses the fat with flavor and aroma, which enhances the oysters. To bump up the citrus notes, try adding 1½ tsp ground sumac to the flavored butter before you broil the oysters.

In a medium saucepan over medium-high heat, melt the butter. Transfer ¾ cup [180 ml] of the melted butter to a blender for later use. Add the shallots to the remaining butter in the saucepan and sauté until translucent, 3 to 4 minutes. Add the bread crumbs and cook, stirring, for about 1 minute, until lightly browned. Remove from the heat and set aside.

Add the cilantro, mint, serrano chile, Aleppo pepper, salt, black pepper, and lemon juice to the melted butter in the blender and pulse until completely smooth. Transfer to a medium bowl and stir in the sautéed shallot and bread crumb mixture.

Remove the hot roasting pan from the oven and turn on the broiler. Arrange the oysters over the salt and place a generous Tbsp of the herbed bread crumb mixture atop each one. Sprinkle a generous tsp of the grated Parmesan over each oyster, and broil the oysters until the bread crumbs have turned golden brown, 3 to 4 minutes. Serve the oysters immediately with the lemon wedges, if desired.

Smoked Sardines and Kumquat Crostini

Crostini look fancy, but they're dead easy to make. And you can top them with anything you like. I make a salty, umami-filled topping of sardines or anchovy fillets paired with thin slices of sweet-tart kumquats, creamy butter beans, fresh dill, and lemon. You could also serve this topping as a dip for the bread.

MAKES 6 TO 8 SERVINGS

½ cup [55 g] kumquats, seeded and thinly sliced

2 Thai chiles, seeded and thinly sliced

¼ cup [45 g] minced shallot

½ cup [5 g] fresh dill fronds

One 15 oz [430 g] can butter beans, drained

One 4¼ oz [120 g] can sardines packed in olive oil, drained

2 Tbsp fresh lemon juice

2 Tbsp extra-virgin olive oil, plus extra for brushing the bread and drizzling

½ tsp fine sea salt

½ tsp freshly ground black pepper

1 whole-wheat or other whole-grain baguette, preferably sourdough

Combine all the ingredients except the bread in a medium bowl. Carefully fold the ingredients together with a large spoon or spatula. Taste and adjust the seasoning. Cover the bowl with plastic wrap and refrigerate for about 30 minutes before serving.

Meanwhile, preheat the oven to 350°F [180°C]. Cut the bread into ¼ in [6 mm] thick slices and brush them lightly on both sides with olive oil. Toast in the oven for about 15 minutes, rotating halfway through baking. Cool the bread for 5 minutes. To serve, top each slice of bread with a generous Tbsp of the topping and drizzle with a little olive oil, if desired.

THE APPROACH Citrus, fresh herbs, and seafood create a symphony of sweet, acidic, and umami elements, which work well together. It's no wonder that these ingredients are often combined in coastal cuisines across the world. Since the kumquats are thinly sliced, the tartness of their flesh tastes less intense. The candylike sweetness of their skin plays off deliciously against the salty pieces of fish. The dill fronds add a hint of freshness, while the Thai chiles add small bursts of unexpected heat to each bite.

Curry Leaf Popcorn Chicken

My husband, Michael, grew up on a farm in the Deep South, and he taught me to love fried chicken. But I learned to make this dish from our dear friend Regina Pearce, who always shakes the chicken (or even shrimp) in small batches in resealable plastic bags to get a uniform coating of flour. Her method has never failed me.

MAKES 4 SERVINGS

Seeds from 4 green cardamom pods

2 tsp coriander seeds

2 tsp cumin seeds

12 black peppercorns

2 cups [480 ml] buttermilk

2 to 3 serrano chiles, seeded, if desired

6 scallions (white and green parts)

30 curry leaves, preferably fresh

4 garlic cloves, peeled

1½ tsp cayenne pepper

One 1 in [2.5 cm] piece fresh ginger, peeled and chopped

¼ cup [60 ml] fresh lime juice

1 Tbsp plus 1 tsp fine sea salt

2 lb [910 g] boneless, skinless chicken breast

2 cups [280 g] all-purpose flour

1 tsp baking powder

½ tsp baking soda

3 cups [720 ml] neutral-tasting oil

4 green Thai chiles, seeded, if desired

Spiced Maple-Vinegar Syrup (page 200), Hot Green Chutney (page 277), or your favorite hot sauce for serving

Heat a small, dry skillet over medium-high heat. Add the cardamom, coriander, cumin seeds, and the peppercorns, and toast for 30 to 45 seconds, swirling the mixture occasionally until the seeds release their aroma and start to brown. Divide the toasted spice mixture in half. Transfer one half of this mixture to a spice grinder and pulse to a fine powder. (You can prepare the spices up to 1 week in advance and store in an airtight container in a cool, dark place.)

THE APPROACH Whenever I make popcorn chicken or fry larger serving pieces, I flavor the dish in stages. The whole spices are toasted to activate their oils. These are then blended into buttermilk to create a savory marinade. More seasoning is then added to the flour in the dredging mixture, and finally, the hot little nuggets of chicken are topped with crunchy fried curry leaves and chile peppers. While we often eat this with a hot sauce or ranch dressing, the very best accompaniment is the maple-vinegar syrup or green chutney.

In a blender, combine the remaining toasted spice mixture with the buttermilk, serrano chiles, scallions, 15 of the curry leaves, the garlic, 1 tsp of the cayenne, the ginger, lime juice, and 1 Tbsp of the salt. Pulse until completely smooth and transfer to a large resealable plastic bag. Pat the chicken breasts dry with paper towels. Trim excess fat from the chicken, and cut the flesh into 1 in [2.5 cm] cubes. Add to the marinade. Seal the bag and shake to coat evenly. Refrigerate for 4 hours.

Meanwhile, prepare the dredging mixture. In a large resealable plastic bag, combine the remaining half of the ground spice mixture with the flour, baking powder, baking soda, remaining ½ tsp cayenne, and remaining 1 tsp salt, shaking vigorously to blend. Finely chop 10 of the remaining curry leaves and add them to the dredging mixture. Seal the bag and shake again to mix well.

Once the chicken has marinated, use tongs to lift out half the chicken pieces, shaking off the excess batter, and transfer to the bag with the dredging mixture. Seal the bag and shake to coat evenly. Transfer the chicken pieces to a wire rack. Repeat with the remaining chicken.

In a medium Dutch oven, heat the oil over medium-high heat to 350°F [180°C]. Fry the chicken in batches, turning occasionally, until golden brown and cooked through, 4 to 5 minutes. Using a slotted spoon or a spider, transfer the chicken to paper towels to drain.

After the chicken is cooked, prepare the garnish: Cut the Thai chiles in half lengthwise. In the hot oil left in the pot, deep-fry the chiles and remaining 5 curry leaves until crispy, 30 to 40 seconds. Drain on paper towels.

Put the chicken on a serving plate, garnish with the chiles and fried curry leaves, and serve hot with the maple-vinegar sauce or hot sauce.

Spiced Beef Kebabs

One of my most vivid memories of going to college in Bombay was heading out with my friends late at night to eat kebabs. Once or twice a week, we'd drive to the south side of the city and enjoy a feast of hot, succulent pieces of seasoned beef, chicken, or lamb, served with thin flatbreads and fresh chutney. *Shami* kebabs are usually made with ground lamb or beef, dried herbs, and chickpea flour for the binding agent; they don't require skewers and are cooked in large flat-bottomed woks. This recipe is inspired by the *shami* kebabs. Serve them with pickled red onions, Hot Green Chutney (page 277), or raita (page 63).

MAKES 7 SERVINGS

1 lb [455 g] ground beef (15 percent fat)

1 cup [140 g] finely diced onion

1 large egg, lightly beaten

½ cup [60 g] chickpea flour

2 Thai chiles, seeded, if desired, and minced

2 garlic cloves, minced

One 1 in [2.5 cm] piece fresh ginger, peeled and grated

1 Tbsp fresh lime juice

1 tsp cayenne pepper

1 tsp coriander seeds, coarsely ground

1 tsp dried mint

½ tsp ground cinnamon

½ tsp dried sage

½ tsp dried dill

½ tsp fine sea salt

½ cup [120 ml] neutral-tasting vegetable oil

2 Tbsp fresh cilantro leaves

Red Onions with Coriander (page 274)

In a large bowl, mix the beef, onion, egg, chickpea flour, chiles, garlic, ginger, lime juice, cayenne, coriander, mint, cinnamon, sage, dill, and salt. Divide into fourteen equal parts and shape into 1 in [2.5 cm] disks.

Heat about 2 Tbsp of the oil in a large cast-iron or nonstick skillet over medium-high heat. Fry the kebabs in batches, adding more oil as needed, until golden brown, 3 to 4 minutes per side. Drain on paper towels. Transfer the kebabs to a serving plate, garnish with the cilantro, and serve with the pickled red onions.

THE APPROACH When making kebabs (or even burgers, for that matter), I often prefer dried herbs because they contain very little to no water and are more potent in flavor than their fresh counter-parts. Here the coriander enhances the heat of the chile peppers.

Crispy Pork Belly Bites

When I eat out in Chinatown in San Francisco or Oakland, I always order pork belly. The crisp outer skin coated with a sweet-and-sour glaze encases meltingly tender meat within. Pure heaven. Here's my version of that dish.

MAKES 6 TO 8 SERVINGS

2 lb [910 g] pork belly

¼ cup [50 g] sugar

¼ cup [65 g] kosher salt

2 Tbsp fresh rosemary leaves, or 2 tsp dried

1 Tbsp fennel seeds

1 tsp black peppercorns

Seeds from one 1 in [2.5 cm] piece vanilla bean pod

Coconut Vinegar–Ginger Glaze

½ cup [120 ml] coconut vinegar

½ cup [100 g] packed jaggery or muscovado sugar

One 1 in [2.5 cm] piece fresh ginger, peeled and grated

Pat the pork belly dry with paper towels and put it in a dish or pan. Mix the sugar and salt in a small bowl and rub both sides of the pork with the mixture. Cover with plastic wrap and refrigerate for at least 6 hours, but no more than 12 hours.

Unwrap the pork belly, rinse off the sugar and salt, and pat dry. In a spice grinder, grind the rosemary, fennel seeds, peppercorns, and vanilla beans to a fine powder. Rub the seasoning over the meaty side of the belly. Return to the baking dish, cover, and refrigerate for 1½ hours.

Preheat the oven to 250°F [120°C]. Place the seasoned pork belly, fat-side up, in a large roasting pan and cook for 2 hours. The top should be lightly browned. Remove the pan from the oven and cool completely, about 2 hours, to allow the pork to firm up. Preheat the broiler. Cut the pork belly into 1 in [2.5 cm] pieces and return the pieces to the roasting pan. Broil until the skin starts to turn puffy and crispy, 4 to 5 minutes. Remove from the oven and, using tongs, transfer the pork belly to a serving dish, discarding any liquid left behind.

THE APPROACH My friend Ben Mims, who was the test kitchen director at Lucky Peach, showed me how to crisp up pork belly by using a mix of salt and sugar to draw out its moisture. Vanilla might seem like an odd flavor for a savory dish, but with fattier cuts of meat, like pork, and a fruity sweet-and-sour glaze like this one, it makes perfect sense.

To make the glaze: While the pork belly is cooking, in a small saucepan, combine the coconut vinegar, jaggery, and ginger. Bring to a rolling boil, lower the heat, and simmer gently until the liquid has reduced by almost half, 8 to 10 minutes. Remove from the heat and keep warm until the pork belly is done. Brush each piece generously with the warm glaze on the crispy top side. Serve warm.

CHAPTER 2: **Salads + Soups**

My favorite salads surprise with their unexpected taste and texture. For example, fruits, with their sweet and acidic notes, stand out well against leafy greens like lettuce or kale, so I combine them. I choose dressings that bring all the elements of the salad into careful balance or heighten the flavors of one or two key ingredients.

I always keep a few acidic items on hand for my salads, including lemons and limes for their juice and zest, South Asian tamarind, and a variety of different vinegars. Sweeteners like jaggery or muscovado sugar are crucial, and so are different types of red chili flakes, including the smoky *urfa biber* (*biber* is the Turkish word for "pepper"). I like to stock my pantry with dried seaweed, too, so I can crumble it into a salad for a little umami.

Soups are about comfort. As one-pot meals they can be real time-savers, and they're a great way to use up leftovers and odds and ends in the refrigerator or pantry. The most satisfying soups have a good balance of acidity and salt, with umami and heat playing supporting roles.

While it might seem a little daunting at first, it's really easy to take a very simple soup and make it your own once you have an idea of how hot, sour, or sweet you want it to be. Take, for example, chicken noodle soup: I like a bold and flavorful broth with a splash of lemon juice and the comforting aroma of sautéed celery. So, I start by playing with the citrus. I might smoke the lemons before adding them to the broth, or perhaps I'll reach for a dried Omani lime, which is used in Persian cooking and adds a hint of earthiness along with its smoky profile. Other times I'll flavor the broth with sautéed pancetta, Bacon-Guajillo Salt (page 267), or a little Roasted Garlic (page 259). These personal choices keep my soups interesting and make the end result different from other soups out there. Keep your pantry well stocked so you, too, can play with soup bases.

Toasted Cumin and Lime Cucumber Salad

In the summer, when I was a kid, I'd eat thick slices of cucumber seasoned with chili flakes, salt, and a splash of lime juice. It was all I needed to stay cool. This is my grown-up version of that childhood snack, which I often serve with spicy meals.

MAKES 4 TO 6 SERVINGS

1 tsp cumin seeds

2 large English cucumbers (1⅓ lb [605 g] total), peeled and diced

1 to 2 green Thai chiles, seeded, if desired, and minced

6 or 7 fresh mint leaves

½ tsp fine sea salt

½ tsp freshly ground black pepper

2 Tbsp fresh lime juice

Heat a small skillet over medium-high heat, add the cumin seeds, and toast until the seeds are fragrant and begin to turn brown, 30 to 45 seconds, swirling the seeds occasionally so they toast evenly. With a mortar and pestle or a spice grinder, grind to a coarse powder. Transfer to a large bowl and add the cucumbers and chiles.

Stack the mint leaves, roll them into a tight cylinder, and cut into thin strips. Add to the bowl along with the salt, pepper, and lime juice. Stir gently to combine. Taste and adjust the seasoning, if necessary. Cover the bowl with plastic wrap and refrigerate for 5 to 10 minutes before serving. This salad is best eaten the day it is made.

THE APPROACH The chiles and cumin add a warm and unexpected contrast to the cool cucumber, mint, and lime juice. Toasting the cumin seeds releases their aromatic oils and gives off a smoky perfume. Once the seeds are ground to a powder, their flavors can permeate the cucumber. It is best to prepare the cumin the day you make the salad, or it will lose its potency.

Caprese Salad with Sweet Tamarind Dressing

I've always enjoyed the Italian caprese because of the way acidic tomatoes play against the sweet-and-sour flavors of aged balsamic and the fruity notes of olive oil. Then there's the beautiful contrast in texture between the soft and creamy mozzarella and the firmer slices of tomatoes. I've reinvented this classic by adding a dressing of tamarind and jaggery.

MAKES 4 SERVINGS

Tamarind Dressing

2 oz [55 g] sour tamarind pulp or paste

½ cup [120 ml] boiling water

¼ cup [60 ml] extra-virgin olive oil

½ tsp fresh lime juice

1 Tbsp jaggery or muscovado sugar

½ tsp ground coriander seeds

½ tsp fine sea salt

½ tsp dried *urfa biber* chili flakes or dried Aleppo pepper flakes

¼ tsp freshly ground black pepper

Salad

1 pt [295 g] cherry tomatoes, halved lengthwise

1 pt [345 g] grape tomatoes, halved lengthwise

4 to 6 plum tomatoes, halved lengthwise

8 oz [230 g] fresh mozzarella bocconcini, cut crosswise into four pieces

3 Tbsp fresh cilantro leaves

1 Tbsp extra-virgin olive oil

½ tsp fine sea salt

To make the dressing: Put the tamarind pulp in a heat-proof bowl and cover with the boiling water. Cover and let sit for at least 1 hour. Massage and squeeze the pulp or paste to soften. Press through a fine-mesh strainer suspended over a small bowl, discarding the solids left behind in the strainer. Put the strained tamarind in a blender and add the olive oil, lime juice, jaggery, coriander, salt, *urfa biber*, and black pepper. Pulse on high speed until well combined. Taste and adjust the sweetness and seasoning, if necessary.

To make the salad: Put the tomatoes in a large bowl and add the mozzarella, cilantro, olive oil, and salt. Add half the tamarind dressing and toss gently to coat evenly. Serve with the extra tamarind dressing on the side.

THE APPROACH While the success of this salad is dependent on good-quality seasonal tomatoes and fresh mozzarella, the tamarind dressing makes the biggest impact on its flavor. Blending the tamarind and olive oil with whole spices releases an irresistible combination of sweet, sour, and earthy flavors into the dressing.

Rainbow Root Raita

Raita is the original savory yogurt bowl, which functions as a salad or a condiment. Throughout my youth, my parents used to serve chilled bowls of fresh creamy yogurt with cucumbers, carrots, beets, or even smashed boiled potatoes folded in, for a salad with plenty of texture and character. It was always one of my favorite parts of the meal. This raita celebrates the different colors of root vegetables. It can be enjoyed as a main course or a side and is the perfect accompaniment to spicy or hot dishes, such as Roast Leg of Lamb (page 181) or Eggplant Pilaf (page 102).

MAKES 6 TO 8 SERVINGS AS A SIDE

2 cups [480 g] plain full-fat yogurt

1 cup [240 ml] cold water

1 tsp fine sea salt

½ tsp ground white pepper

½ cup [35 g] peeled and grated carrot

½ cup [50 g] peeled and grated golden beets (see The Approach)

½ cup [50 g] peeled and grated red beets

2 Tbsp thinly sliced scallion (white and green parts)

1 Tbsp neutral-tasting vegetable oil

½ tsp black mustard seeds

5 to 6 curry leaves, preferably fresh

½ tsp grated peeled fresh ginger

In a large bowl, whisk together the yogurt, water, salt, and pepper. Taste and adjust the seasoning, if necessary. Add the grated vegetables and the scallions, but don't mix them just yet.

In a small skillet, heat the oil over medium-high heat. Add the mustard seeds and curry leaves (be careful, as the mustard seeds will sizzle and pop when they hit the hot oil). Swirl the oil gently until the seeds stop sizzling and the leaves crisp up but are still green, 30 to 45 seconds. Remove from the heat and add the ginger to the hot oil, stirring for 10 to 15 seconds. Pour the seasoned oil mixture with the seeds, leaves, and ginger over the yogurt and vegetables in the bowl and stir just until blended. (Avoid overmixing or the red beet color will turn the entire dish pink.) Serve immediately.

THE APPROACH Here I use the Indian technique of *tadka*, or tempering (page 161). Hot oil is infused with spices and aromatics before it's poured over the yogurt, adding texture as well as flavor to this yogurt-based salad. Golden beets can darken when grated and exposed to air. To prevent this, add a few drops of lemon or lime juice (about 1 or 2 tsp per ½ cup [50 g] of grated beets).

Roasted Cauliflower, Paneer, and Mixed Lentil Salad

With its soft, creamy texture, paneer (an Indian cottage cheese made by curdling boiling milk with lemon juice) is excellent in salads. And it has an interesting quality: it holds its shape when heated, and doesn't melt. Here it's roasted with cauliflower.

MAKES 7 TO 8 SERVINGS AS A SIDE

½ cup [100 g] green lentils, picked over for stones

½ cup [115 g] black lentils, picked over for stones

1 small cauliflower (1 lb [455 g])

10 oz [280 g] Paneer (page 260), cut into ½ in [12 mm] cubes (about 2 cups)

1 tsp fine sea salt

½ tsp freshly ground black pepper

1 Tbsp extra-virgin olive oil

4 scallions, thinly sliced (white and green parts)

¼ cup [60 g] Cilantro Oil Dressing (page 278)

Preheat the oven to 425°F [220°C]. Rinse the lentils in a fine-mesh strainer under cold running water. Transfer to a medium saucepan and add enough water to cover by about 1 in [2.5 cm]. Bring to a rolling boil over medium-high heat, turn the heat to low, and simmer, uncovered, until tender but not mushy, 30 to 60 minutes. The cooking time will vary depending on how old the lentils are, so check them every 5 minutes after the first half hour. Drain through a fine-mesh strainer and set on a clean kitchen towel to absorb any remaining liquid.

While the lentils are cooking, roast the cauliflower and paneer: Break the cauliflower into bite-size florets and transfer to a roasting pan. Add the paneer. Season with the salt and pepper and drizzle with the olive oil, mixing to coat evenly. Roast, stirring occasionally, until the florets and paneer are crispy on the outside and feel tender when pierced with a skewer or knife, 20 to 25 minutes. Transfer to a large bowl and gently stir in the drained lentils and scallions. Taste and adjust the seasoning, if necessary. Drizzle with the dressing and serve warm or at room temperature. (Store the left-over salad in an airtight container in the refrigerator for up to 4 days.)

THE APPROACH In this warm salad, the cauliflower florets and little cubes of paneer are tossed with olive oil and then roasted until they're charred and crispy outside, while remaining soft and tender within. Because the flavors are rather earthy, the cilantro dressing coats the paneer and vegetables with a fresh and herbaceous flavor.

Chouriço Potato Salad

I love salads that can be served in any season, at any time of day. This one is great for breakfast with a couple of fried eggs, or in a taco, or by itself for lunch. It's bursting with flavor from my Goan-style *chouriço*.

MAKES 4 SERVINGS

8 oz [230 g] *chouriço*, homemade (page 191) or store-bought

2 Tbsp extra-virgin olive oil

1½ lb [680 g] fingerling potatoes, halved lengthwise

1 tsp fine sea salt

½ tsp freshly ground black pepper

1 tsp ground chipotle chile

½ tsp paprika

2 Tbsp raw pumpkin seeds (pepitas)

1 Tbsp thinly sliced chives

¼ cup [65 g] crumbled Paneer (page 260)

2 Tbsp fresh cilantro leaves, plus more for garnish

¼ cup [60 ml] fresh lime juice

1 lime, quartered, for garnish (optional)

If you purchased the *chouriço*, remove from the casing. Break the meat into small pieces and set aside. Heat the olive oil in a large skillet over medium-high heat. Add the potatoes and sprinkle with the salt and black pepper. Cook, stirring occasionally, until the potatoes are tender, 5 to 6 minutes. Sprinkle with the chipotle chile and paprika and fold to coat evenly. Add the *chouriço* and cook for another 4 to 5 minutes, or until the sausage is browned and cooked through, stirring frequently. Add the pumpkin seeds and cook for 1 minute longer. Remove the pan from the heat and transfer the contents to a large bowl. Cool for 5 minutes.

Gently stir the chives, paneer, cilantro, and lime juice into the warm potatoes. Taste and adjust the seasoning, if necessary. Garnish with fresh cilantro leaves, and serve warm or at room temperature with lime wedges, if desired.

THE APPROACH A lot of the flavor in this dish comes from the *chouriço*. The pork fat and the smoky combination of paprika, cumin, and chiles make this salad pop. To counterbalance the spiciness of the *chouriço*, I fold in paneer, cilantro, and lime juice, which are cooling. If you like, swap in a little crumbled Cotija or queso fresco for the paneer.

Butternut Squash and Tea Soup

Even a vegan soup like this one can boast rich umami flavors. During the fall, when pumpkins and butternut squash are in season, I make a large pot of this warm elixir. Infusing the broth with dried shiitake mushrooms and smoky Lapsang Souchong tea leaves gives this soup a deep, "meaty" profile. Add the squash ribbons just before serving so they don't become limp.

MAKES 2 TO 4 SERVINGS

1 small butternut squash (1½ lb [680 g])

4 cups [960 ml] water

12 black peppercorns

4 garlic cloves, peeled

One 2 in [5 cm] piece fresh ginger, peeled and sliced

2 star anise pods

4 dried shiitake mushrooms

2 tsp Lapsang Souchong tea leaves

1 Tbsp soy sauce

1 Tbsp fresh lemon juice

½ tsp fine sea salt

2 Tbsp toasted sesame oil

3 Tbsp fresh cilantro leaves

Trim the ends of the butternut squash. Halve lengthwise and remove the seeds. Peel the skin and, using the peeler, cut the flesh lengthwise into thin ribbons. Put the ribbons in a bowl of ice water until ready to use.

Combine the 4 cups [960 ml] water, peppercorns, garlic, ginger, star anise, and shiitakes in a medium stockpot or Dutch oven. Bring to a rolling boil over medium-high heat. Turn the heat to low and simmer, uncovered, for 20 minutes. Put the tea leaves in a tea infuser or a muslin spice bag and add to the pot. Increase the heat to high and boil for 30 seconds. Remove and discard the tea leaves.

Place a fine-mesh strainer over a large bowl and strain the broth, discarding the solids. Return the broth to the stockpot and add the soy sauce, lemon juice, and salt. Taste and adjusting the seasoning, if necessary. Keep warm until ready to serve.

Just before serving, remove the squash ribbons from the ice water, pat them dry with paper towels, and transfer to the warm broth. Stir in the sesame oil, garnish with the fresh cilantro leaves, and serve.

THE APPROACH Avoid adding too much tea to the soup or steeping it for too long, or it will taste bitter. Choose a dark sesame oil for greater depth of flavor. Thinly sliced scallions are also a great garnish for this soup.

Cocoa-Spiced Bean and Lentil Soup

I keep many different dried beans and lentils in my pantry, and this soup gives me a chance to mix up any stragglers in a single pot. Serve it in the coldest depths of winter, and start it one day ahead to allow time for the beans to soak overnight.

MAKES 4 SERVINGS

¾ cup [135 g] mixed dried beans (such as kidney, black, and cranberry), picked over for stones

¼ cup [50 g] mixed lentils and split peas, picked over for stones

1 Tbsp Ghee (page 268) or extra-virgin olive oil

1 cup [140 g] finely diced onion

2 garlic cloves, minced

2 Tbsp unsweetened cocoa powder

1 tsp ground coriander

1 tsp Kashmiri chile powder

½ tsp ground mace

One 14½ oz [415 g] can chopped tomatoes, with their juices

4 cups [960 ml] water

1 tsp fine sea salt

10 fresh mint leaves

¼ cup [60 g] plain Greek yogurt

Rinse the beans in a fine-mesh strainer under cold running water and transfer to a medium bowl. Cover with 2 in [5 cm] of water and soak overnight. The next day, rinse the beans and lentils in a fine-mesh strainer under cold running water and transfer to a small bowl. Cover with 2 in [5 cm] of water and soak for at least 1 hour before cooking. Drain the beans and lentils.

Heat the ghee in a medium Dutch oven or stockpot over medium-high heat. Sauté the onion until translucent, 4 to 5 minutes. Add the garlic and cook until fragrant, 30 to 45 seconds. Stir in the cocoa, coriander, chile, and mace and cook until aromatic, about 30 seconds. Pour in the tomatoes and their juices and cook for 3 to 4 minutes. Add the 4 cups [960 ml] water and salt and stir. Increase the heat to high and bring to a rolling boil. Turn the heat to low, cover, and simmer gently until the beans and lentils are soft and tender, about 1 hour. Taste and adjust the seasoning, if necessary.

Meanwhile, stack the mint leaves, roll them into a tight cylinder, and cut into thin strips. Serve the soup hot, garnishing each bowl with 1 Tbsp of the Greek yogurt and a few ribbons of mint.

THE APPROACH Beans and lentils are comfort food, mainly because of their creamy, soft textures once cooked. Just as cocoa adds depth to a mole sauce in Mexican cooking, it works wonders here, bringing complexity, color, and a pleasant, subtle bitterness. The heat of the ground chile and the fragrance of the mace add to the sensory delight of this soup. A cool garnish of creamy yogurt and fresh mint provides a welcome contrast.

Toasted Naan and Chicken Soup

If Indians had a version of chicken tortilla soup, this would be it. Make a large pot on the weekend to eat during the week. Trust me, the flavors will keep getting better with each passing day.

MAKES 4 TO 6 SERVINGS

Seeds of 2 green cardamom pods

4 Tbsp [60 ml] extra-virgin olive oil

1 cup [140 g] finely diced red onion

2 garlic cloves, peeled and minced

1 tsp ground Kashmiri chile

½ tsp ground turmeric

1 tsp garam masala, homemade (page 263) or store-bought

One 14½ oz [415 g] can chopped tomatoes, with their juices

2 cups [250 g] shredded cooked chicken

4 cups [960 ml] low-sodium chicken broth

1 cup [140 g] raw sweet corn, fresh or frozen

3 Tbsp fresh lime juice

½ tsp fine sea salt

2 Naans (page 94)

4 Hard-Boiled Eggs (page 255), peeled and halved lengthwise

3 Tbsp fresh cilantro leaves

2 Tbsp thinly sliced scallion (white and green parts)

1 serrano chile, seeded, if desired, and thinly sliced

Preheat the oven to 350°F [180°C]. Grind the cardamom seeds with a mortar and pestle or spice grinder. Heat 2 Tbsp of the oil in a medium stockpot or Dutch oven over medium-high heat. Add the onion and sauté until translucent, 4 to 5 minutes. Turn the heat to medium-low and add the garlic, cardamom, ground chile, turmeric, and garam masala and cook until fragrant, 30 to 45 seconds. Add the tomatoes with their juices and cook, stirring occasionally, for 3 to 4 minutes. Stir in the chicken and cook for 2 minutes. Pour in the chicken broth and add the corn and lime juice. Increase the heat to high and bring to a rolling boil. Turn the heat to low, cover, and simmer gently until the corn is tender, 10 to 12 minutes. Stir in the salt and taste and adjust the seasoning if necessary. Let the soup sit, covered, for 10 minutes before serving.

THE APPROACH The soup base is built the traditional way, by sautéing the aromatics (onion and garlic) and the spices to help release their essential oils and mellow their flavors. The ground Kashmiri chile gives this soup a deep red color without making it too hot. Though garam masala already contains some cardamom, I've added a bit extra to highlight its taste.

You can also make this into an egg-drop soup: Leave out the hard-boiled eggs, and just before serving, bring the soup to a rolling boil. With a fork, stir 2 lightly beaten eggs into the soup to form threads. Serve with the remaining garnishes.

While the soup is cooking, cut the naan into ¼ in [6 mm] wide strips, drizzle with the remaining 2 Tbsp oil. Toast on a baking sheet in the oven until golden brown and crisp, 8 to 10 minutes. Remove from the oven and cool for 5 minutes.

Reheat the soup, if necessary. Garnish with the toasted naan strips, hard-boiled eggs, cilantro, scallion, and serrano chile. Serve hot.

Chicken Noodle Soup with Omani Limes

We home cooks tend to have a repertoire of recipes we make often and adapt to suit our own needs and tastes. Here is one recipe from my own collection. It arose out of necessity, when I didn't have enough lime juice to flavor the broth of my chicken noodle soup. I instead used a few dried Omani limes I unearthed in my pantry.

MAKES 4 TO 6 SERVINGS

1 Tbsp extra-virgin olive oil

½ cup [70 g] finely diced white onion

½ cup [70 g] finely diced carrot

½ cup [60 g] finely diced celery

4 dried Omani limes

½ tsp freshly ground black pepper

⅛ tsp ground turmeric

1 lb [455 g] bone-in chicken breast, skin removed

½ tsp fine sea salt

2 Tbsp fresh lime juice

6 cups [1.4 L] water

2 oz [55 g] dried egg noodles

2 Tbsp fresh flat-leaf parsley leaves

Heat the olive oil in a medium stockpot or Dutch oven over medium-high heat. Add the onion, carrot, and celery and sauté until the carrot is tender, 10 to 12 minutes. Poke a few holes in the Omani limes, which will allow the liquid to penetrate the limes and draw out their flavor as they cook in the broth. Toss them into the pot. Add the black pepper and turmeric and cook for 45 to 60 seconds. Add the chicken, salt, lime juice, and water and increase the heat to high. Bring to a rolling boil. Turn the heat to low, cover, and simmer gently until the chicken is cooked through, about 20 minutes. Using tongs, remove the chicken and carefully shred it with a fork, discarding the bones. Return the chicken to the pot and add the noodles. Continue simmering until the noodles are tender, 6 to 8 minutes. Taste and adjust the seasoning, if necessary. Garnish with the fresh parsley leaves.

THE APPROACH This is a good place to use bone-in chicken parts. The bones give the broth a rich, deep flavor. Omani limes (*limu Omani*) are sold whole and ground and are used often in Persian cooking. While they're cooking, they release an earthy, tangy flavor that's more complex than that of a fresh lime, elevating this simple chicken noodle soup to a whole new level.

Bone and Lentil Broth

As a kid, I'd spend Thursdays at my maternal grandparents' home, watching my grandmother Lucy cook. If I behaved, she let me help. Among the things I learned from her was the importance of cutting vegetables to the same shape and size when preparing the mirepoix for a bone broth. She usually made her bone broth from beef or mutton bones and often threw in a handful of lentils or alphabet noodles for extra body. This broth takes its cues from my Nana and is as rich and flavorful as I remember hers to be.

MAKES 4 SERVINGS

2½ to 3 lb [1.2 to 1.4 kg] beef or lamb bones

2 Tbsp Ghee (page 268)

1 cup [140 g] finely diced onion

1 cup [110 g] finely diced celery

½ cup [70 g] finely diced carrot

2 garlic cloves, minced

2 bay leaves, fresh or dried

5 whole cloves

1 Tbsp freshly ground black pepper

1 tsp ground Kashmiri chile

½ tsp ground turmeric

4½ cups [1 L] water

¼ cup [50 g] red lentils, picked over for stones

2 Tbsp cider vinegar or fresh lemon juice

1 Tbsp fine sea salt

1 Tbsp chopped fresh flat-leaf parsley leaves

Put the bones in a medium stockpot or Dutch oven and cover with cold water. Bring to a rolling boil over high heat. Turn the heat to medium-low and simmer for 20 minutes, skimming off any foam that rises to the surface.

While the bones are blanching, preheat the oven to 450°F [230°C]. Transfer the blanched bones to a cast-iron baking dish or a roasting pan and roast in the hot oven until the meat attached to the bones is crisp and dark brown, about 30 minutes.

Wash and dry the Dutch oven. Add the ghee and heat over medium-high heat. Add the onion, celery, and carrot and sauté until they begin to brown, 10 to 12 minutes. Add the garlic and cook for 1 minute. Add the bay leaves, cloves, pepper, Kashmiri chile, and turmeric and cook until fragrant, 30 to 45 seconds.

THE APPROACH A couple of tips from my friend Andy Barghani, the senior test kitchen editor at the *Bon Appétit* kitchen, in New York City, who helped me improve this recipe. Andy recommended blanching the bones in water to remove any impurities, which also helps remove much of the cloudiness that develops in a bone broth (a technique also used for preparing a consommé). To add more depth, he suggested roasting the blanched bones at a temperature high enough to caramelize the proteins. The spices I've added to the broth accentuate the soup's umami flavors even more.

Return the roasted bones to the pot, scraping in any browned bits from the pan. Pour the 4½ cups [1 L] water over the bones. Rinse the lentils in a fine-mesh strainer under cold running water and add to the pot. Increase the heat to high and bring to a boil. Turn the heat to low and add the vinegar and salt. Cover and simmer until the lentils are falling-apart tender, about 2 hours. Discard the bay leaves. Garnish with the chopped parsley and serve hot.

Bombay, like most large cosmopolitan cities, is over-populated, and apartment sizes seem to be constantly shrinking to keep up with the growing demand for housing. My parents' condominium was modest. We had a tiny kitchen, but to a child curious about food, it was a fascinating place where all the magic happened. Stacked in a wall cabinet were two shelves devoted to my mother's small collection of dried spices, which she stored in neatly labeled jam jars and plastic containers. To a budding cook and scientist, it was a fully stocked lab.

My mother kept a small collection of cookbooks and newspaper cuttings in a drawer. From the time I was twelve years old, I'd spend my summer holidays going through them and attempting to cook some of the dishes, both savory and sweet. These would usually end up as disasters, like the time I thought it would be a good idea to a make a cake with the whole-wheat flour we used to make rotis (a type of Indian flatbread). The result was a cake tough enough to be a doorstopper. Or the time I thought lime juice would taste good in my scrambled eggs (they curdled before they even hit the pan). While I had quite a few failures early on, I paid attention to what worked and what didn't.

I also spent time watching my mom and grandmother cook, and if I got lucky, they'd let me help them. They based most of their recipes on a template of aromas and taste, which they adjusted to bring out the flavors of the main ingredients in a dish. For example, for most meat dishes, they would start with a bowl of chopped onions and sauté them until translucent. Then they would add a mixture of freshly ground ginger and garlic (Indian cooks often grind ginger and garlic to a smooth paste) and a bit of fresh or dried chiles for heat, a pinch of turmeric and Kashmiri chile powder for color, and some vinegar, yogurt, or lime juice at the end to round off the flavor with their acidity. Sometimes they added other spices for more depth, such as ground green cardamom or cumin or garam masala. They liked to season their dishes with salt and black pepper while they cooked, tasting as they went along.

My dad loved making pickles—both fermented and Indian-style ones—for which he seasoned vegetables and fruits with a mixture of mustard oil and spices. The windowsill in our kitchen was lined with the hot and spicy fruits of his labors—jars of pickled cauliflowers, carrots, mangoes, peppers, lemons, and limes. Since edible-grade mustard oil is not legally sold in America, some of these pickles are hard to re-create, but I've worked out a recipe for a lemon pickle packed in olive oil (page 274) that is as flavorful and tasty as my dad's. And it's made with ingredients found easily in the West.

Keeping It Fresh

My parents followed a few rules: Buy as much as you need, and no more. Don't store most of your spices for more than four to six months. When using a ground spice, if possible, grind it yourself in small quantities so that it's fresh. They made an exception for Garam Masala (page 263) and Chaat Masala (page 263), which they used frequently and made in large quantities, which would last a month. They stored their fresh herbs and chiles in the refrigerator. The herbs were usually wrapped in a damp paper towel and slipped into a loosely closed plastic bag. This arrangement allowed the herbs to breathe, while the paper towel wicked away the moisture. I noticed these simple habits when I was a kid, and they have helped me in my adult life to become a better cook.

Your Kitchen Is Your Laboratory

Think of your kitchen as a lab. But unlike a pristine and sterile medical lab, your kitchen lab is a place to play and experiment, often with tasty outcomes. It's where you can develop a deeper understanding of the ingredients and spices that go into your food.

It's important to understand your spices and other ingredients before you incorporate them into your cooking. The best way I know to do this is to jump right in. Smell the spice (or ingredient), and taste it. Decide whether it has salty, sour, sweet, bitter, or savory notes. See whether it also produces a cooling or warming sensation. Some foods even evoke pleasant or unpleasant emotions or memories. Whenever I smell freshly grated coconut, I think of the sweet coconut cakes of my childhood.

The seasonings I choose depend on what I'm cooking and on my physiology (the 10,000 taste receptors inside my mouth and the 400 scent receptors in my nose). But my mood also affects the way I cook. There are times when I crave a combination of sweet and salty, while on other occasions, I want some chile heat to liven up a dish.

Although ingredients vary across cultures, they can be broken down into five main groups, which correspond to our taste receptors: salty, sour, sweet, bitter, and savory (umami). Beyond these five tastes, there are other important qualities in the foods we cook with, including heat, aroma, and color. Herbs and fats lend another layer of flavor.

SALTY

Most vegetables, fruits, and meats contain some amount of salt naturally, but we still season our food with salt to round off the taste of a dish. In Indian cooking, besides regular table salt and sea salt, we also use black salt (*kala namak*) and Himalayan pink salt. A lot of ingredients that come from the ocean—seaweed, shellfish, and fish—already contain a significant amount of salt, so I taste carefully when possible before adding more. Salt is one of the easiest ingredients to experiment with.

I often make a couple of different table seasonings with salt (see the Salt Blends on page 267) and keep them in the pantry.

SOUR

Foods with sour notes can cut through monotonous textures or flavors, such as the cloying sweetness of many fruit jams, and add a little depth. Sour tastes leave a pleasant tingling sensation on the tongue. In Indian cuisine, limes are used more often than lemons for savory dishes because they are grown all over India and are easier to find in the markets. I prefer to pair limes with hot chiles in savory dishes because they tend to amplify the heat. Try this yourself: Taste a few red chili flakes with a few drops of fresh lime juice, and then with fresh lemon juice and see which combination is hotter.

Tamarind pulp or paste is often added to curries and stews. Goan cooking often includes coconut vinegar (see the red snapper on page 130), which is made by fermenting the tree's sap. You can find it at most Asian and Indian grocery stores and in many natural food stores. I like the Coconut Secret brand. I also like apple cider vinegar for adding acidity, especially when cooking meat (see the turkey hand pies on page 155) and fish. Some spices have fruity and acidic notes, including sumac (dried ground sumac berries), amchur (ground dried green unripe mango), and anardana (dried pomegranate seeds, whole or ground). They work well with barbecue sauces, stews, and other earthy dishes. Red and white wines are great sources of fruity acid, and so is verjus, the juice of unripe grapes, which like wine is available *blanc* (white) and *rouge* (red). I use wine or verjus when cooking poultry and meat, such as beef stew (page 170). Sour dairy products, such as yogurt and buttermilk, add acidity to a marinade (see the tandoori fish on page 127) and help tenderize meat (see the popcorn chicken on page 48).

SWEET

Like many folks, I have a fondness for sweets, a craving I tend to satisfy often. Indians use a variety of sweeteners when they cook. Jaggery (*gur* in Hindi), a highly impure form of sugar, is my favorite because it is rich in salty and earthy notes, which add a lot of character to foods.

Muscovado sugar is a good substitute, if you can't find jaggery. I also like to use palm sugar, honey, and maple syrup—I'm a tad bit obsessed with adding maple syrup to my Masala Chai (page 264). Beyond sugar, anise and fennel have a licoricelike taste that is slightly sweet. We also tend to associate cinnamon, nutmeg, green cardamom, and vanilla with sweet flavors because we often use them in desserts. But these flavorings aren't sweet themselves.

BITTER

I have a low tolerance for most bitter foods, and I'm not the only one. Some people have a genetic predisposition, which might be an evolutionary remnant that once prevented humans from consuming poisonous foods. Cocoa, coffee, and tea are all naturally bitter, but we like them because they act as stimulants. Many spices have a bitter taste, such as cinnamon.

SAVORY

Also called umami, this meaty taste is produced by glutamate, an amino acid found in meats and tomatoes. Other foods with high levels of glutamate that will make your dishes taste meatier are fish, mushrooms, cabbage, soy sauce, tea, and coffee. For example, although Butternut Squash and Tea Soup (page 70) is vegan, the Lapsang Souchong tea leaves and dried mushrooms give it a rich, meaty flavor. Umami is not a characteristic flavor of Indian cooking.

HOT

That exciting burning sensation you feel when you eat a fresh Thai or serrano chile pepper is a response to the naturally occurring chemical inside the pepper called capsacin. When cooking Indian food, I use serrano chiles for a milder heat and Thai chiles for a hotter dish. I also like guajillo chiles, which are dried, and cayenne pepper. If you want your food to taste less hot, remove the seeds and the central white membrane (the hottest parts of the chile) before adding the chile, fresh or dried, to the dish.

AROMA

When you think about how you want to season your food, consider the aromas that spices and other ingredients impart to a dish. Cinnamon has a sweet, woody scent; turmeric smells earthy; and ghee and sesame seeds lend a nutty aroma. Orange peel imparts a heavenly fruity aroma. (I often add dried orange peel to garam masala to make my house seasoning for steaks on page 173.) For an herbaceous note, try tarragon, and for a floral one, think of orange blossom water or rose water. Vanilla and green cardamom produce a sweet perfume.

COLOR

Some ingredients color food, like a dye. Turmeric adds a yellow tinge to food, such as in the Sweet Potato Bebinca (page 204), while saffron strands contribute a golden-orange color, as in the Jaggery Ice Cream (page 199). Dried kokum fruit, annatto, and beets add reddish or deep pink tones. Kashmiri chile adds a deep red color characteristic of many Indian dishes, such as curries and tandoori fish (page 127). And most fresh herbs, when puréed, will enhance a dish with their green pigments.

HERBS

Fresh herbs are a great way to brighten up any recipe, whether sweet or savory. Use mint to garnish a scoop of chocolate ice cream, and curry leaves to flavor the marinade for popcorn chicken (page 48). Blend tarragon for a savory lassi (page 232). When cooking with dried herbs, use less than you would fresh, as they have a more concentrated flavor.

FATS

No discussion about taste is complete without fats. They are often the first flavor that goes into a dish. When cooking with butter, I use unsalted so I can control the amount of salt in the dish. I use Ghee (page 268) for its nutty aroma and taste and the Ethiopian spiced butter, nit'r qibe (page 270) for its bold flavor profile, which comes from the mixture of spices infused into the fat. The fats from bacon, pancetta, and sausage, when rendered, make flavorful cooking fats. I keep them on hand and often use them to roast vegetables (see the Chouriço Potato Salad on page 69). Duck fat is another good cooking fat that's packed with flavor. When I cook with oil, I usually use walnut or olive oil. I especially like oil made from Arbequina olives, which tastes grassy; from Arbosana, which is floral; and from Koroneiki, which has a pungent flavor. I prefer neutral-tasting oils such as sunflower, canola, and grapeseed when deep-frying or grilling, because they also have higher smoke points.

I learned how to season my food through trial and error. So celebrate your failures as well as your successes. They will make you a better cook, and in the process, you will learn to treat recipes as a template to create your own flavors.

CHAPTER 3: Grains + Vegetables

Vegetarianism is commonplace in India. Though our household was not strictly vegetarian, we ate a lot of whole grains and vegetables of different colors, shapes, and textures. These hearty vegetable and grain dishes were flavorful as well as colorful, and the meats were usually considered more of an accompaniment to the meal.

The key to making grains stand out is to cook and season them well. Often, I'll sauté grains such as rice or wheat berries in a little hot oil or a flavorful fat such as ghee until they're coated, and then add the water or stock. I like to add a bunch of stir-fried vegetables to the cooked grains, or toss the grains with puréed herbs.

Every grain has its own unique shape, color, taste, and aroma, which you will want to consider when cooking. For example, nuttier grains, like wheat berries and kasha, taste great in cold salads. Rice comes in many lovely colors (red, brown, black), as well as shapes. Arborio rice is short, basmati and wild rice are long, and Goa rice is fat. Toasting grains before you cook them brings out their aromas and flavors. Sometimes I'll use a small quantity for texture in a soup or a salad.

When I cook vegetables, I usually braise them in their own liquids or sauté them in hot oil infused with spices. Sometimes, I'll just season and roast them. All three of these methods enhance the flavors of the vegetables, unlike steaming, a technique I don't use very often. Vegetables with a high sugar content, such as carrots and sweet potatoes, become sweeter when exposed to high heat. They also develop appealing bittersweet notes as their sugars caramelize. Heat also helps release the volatile aromatic compounds in whole and ground spices such as coriander and green cardamom. These oils vaporize and permeate the tissues of the vegetables or the liquids they are sitting in, resulting in a more deeply flavored dish.

Granola Two Ways

I like to snack a lot. And by a lot, I mean a crazy amount. I've got jars with random assortments of nuts and dried fruit lining an entire shelf of my pantry. A few years ago, in an effort to be more organized and free up space, I started making granola. Here are two of my favorite recipes: one sweet and one savory.

The sweet granola, spiced with fennel and ginger, is rich in dried fruit and nuts, while the savory version is flavored with sun-dried tomatoes, powdered tomatoes, and smoked paprika. You can find bags of sun-dried tomatoes and jars of tomato powder at many international markets. You can also make your own tomato powder by grinding dehydrated or sun-dried tomatoes with a spice mill or blender.

Fennel and Ginger–Spiced Sweet Granola

MAKES 5 CUPS [635 G]

2 cups [190 g] old-fashioned rolled oats

½ cup [70 g] mixed raisins and dried cranberries

8 dried figs, chopped

2 Tbsp raw sunflower seeds

½ cup [70 g] chopped raw cashews

½ cup [50 g] sliced raw almonds

1 Tbsp poppy seeds

1½ tsp fennel seeds

1½ tsp ground ginger

½ tsp fine sea salt

1 Tbsp apple cider vinegar

½ cup [120 ml] maple syrup

¼ cup [60 ml] extra-virgin olive oil

Preheat the oven to 300°F [150°C]. Line a baking sheet with parchment paper.

In a large bowl, mix together the oats, raisins and cranberries, figs, sunflower seeds, cashews, almonds, poppy seeds, fennel seeds, ginger, and salt. In a medium bowl, whisk together the vinegar, maple syrup, and olive oil and drizzle over the oat mixture. Using your hands or a rubber spatula, gently mix to coat evenly and spread out on the prepared baking sheet in a single layer. Let sit for 20 minutes.

Continued

THE APPROACH To make the sweet granola more interesting, I incorporated fennel seeds and ground ginger. The result is a tasty cereal with pops of licorice and toasty, nutty, gingery flavors.

For the savory granola, I used a mixture of sun-dried tomatoes, tomato powder, and smoky paprika along with garlic and onion powders. The hint of sugar, the acidity from the vinegar, and the tomato flavor remind me of my favorite potato chips. If you want the granola to taste slightly cheesy without adding actual cheese, add 1 or 2 tsp of nutritional yeast when you mix the ingredients together.

The trick to making good granola is to let the oats rest and absorb the flavors you've mixed them with before they're placed in the hot oven. Vinegar helps counterbalance the flavors in each recipe and increase the granola's crunchiness and shelf life.

Bake until the oats are golden brown and crispy, 20 to 25 minutes, stirring every 10 minutes so the oats don't stick together in clumps.

Remove from the oven and place the baking sheet on a cooling rack to cool completely. Store in an airtight container at room temperature for up to 3 weeks.

Savory Granola

MAKES 4 CUPS [410 G]

2 cups [190 g] old-fashioned rolled oats

½ cup [70 g] whole raw cashews

2 Tbsp raw sunflower seeds

1 Tbsp white sesame seeds

1 Tbsp black sesame seeds

1 Tbsp jaggery or brown sugar

1 Tbsp tomato powder

1 tsp smoked paprika

1½ tsp garlic powder

1½ tsp onion powder

1 tsp fine sea salt

½ tsp ground Kashmiri chile

2 Tbsp apple cider vinegar

¼ cup [60 ml] extra-virgin olive oil

¼ cup [25 g] sun-dried cherry tomatoes, coarsely chopped

Preheat the oven to 300°F [150°C]. Line a baking sheet with parchment paper.

In a large bowl, mix together the oats, cashews, sunflower seeds, white and black sesame seeds, jaggery, tomato powder, paprika, garlic and onion powders, salt, and chile until well combined.

In a small bowl, whisk together the vinegar and olive oil and drizzle over the oat mixture. Using your hands or a rubber spatula, gently mix the ingredients to coat evenly and spread out on the prepared baking sheet. Let sit for 20 minutes.

Bake until the oats are golden brown and crispy, 20 to 25 minutes, stirring every 10 minutes. Remove from the oven, stir in the sun-dried tomatoes, and place the baking sheet on a cooling rack to cool completely. Store in an airtight container at room temperature for up to 3 weeks.

Naan

I prefer homemade naan to the dense and doughy store-bought ones. It's so easy to whip up; you just need to plan ahead so the dough has time to rise. I use whole wheat pastry flour to make naan because it contains more fiber than all-purpose flour but less gluten, which helps produce a softer bread.

The naan dough is actually a twofer, because you can use it as a base for flatbread pizza. While the choice of toppings is endless, Margherita pizza (page 99) sprinkled with nigella seeds is my favorite way to eat up all those colorful little tomatoes we grow in our backyard.

MAKES 4 FLATBREADS

½ cup [120 ml] whole milk, heated to 105 to 115°F [41 to 46°C]

1 large egg

2 Tbsp plain full-fat Greek yogurt

1 Tbsp unsalted butter, melted

1 Tbsp sugar

1 tsp fine sea salt

1 Tbsp active dry yeast

2 cups [280 g] all-purpose flour or whole-wheat pastry flour, plus more for rolling out the naans

Using a fork, whisk the milk, egg, yogurt, butter, sugar, and salt in a small bowl. Sprinkle with the yeast and let sit for 5 minutes. The mixture should be bubbly on the surface.

Put the flour in a large bowl or mound on a clean work surface and make a well in the center. Pour the yeast mixture into the middle of the well. Using clean hands or a large wooden spoon, gradually mix the flour from the inside wall of the well into the liquid to form a sticky dough. Knead well for 4 to 5 minutes.

Fold the dough by grabbing it from the underside and stretching it and folding it back over itself. Rotate a quarter of a turn and repeat three or four times. Brush a large bowl with a little oil and put the dough in the bowl. Cover with plastic wrap and allow to rise in a dark, warm place until doubled in size, about 4 hours.

THE APPROACH Naan can be seasoned in many different ways. Instead of garlic, you can try mixing butter or ghee with spices and herbs, such as Aleppo pepper flakes, *urfa biber*, crushed coriander, and oregano.

Divide the dough into four equal parts and shape into balls. On a clean, lightly floured work surface, use a rolling pin to roll out the balls of dough, one at a time, into circles about ⅛ in [4 mm] thick and about 6 in [15 cm] in diameter.

To cook the naan, heat a large skillet with a lid over medium-high heat. Slap a circle of dough into the hot skillet and cover the pan to trap the steam. Cook for 3 to 4 minutes, flip the dough, and turn the heat to low. Cook, covered, until the naan blisters, with a few big bubbles, 1 to 2 minutes. Remove from the pan and wrap in a clean kitchen towel. Repeat with the remaining three circles of dough.

Garlic Naan

Before you cook the naan, in a small bowl, mix ¼ cup [60 ml] melted, unsalted butter or Ghee (page 268) with 1 tsp minced fresh cilantro and 1 grated garlic clove. Cook the naan as above, brushing the mixture over the tops of the hot flatbreads. Cook, one at a time, for an additional 30 seconds. Sprinkle with flaky salt and serve hot.

Margherita Naan Pizza

MAKES 2 INDIVIDUAL PIZZAS

Dough of 1 recipe Naan (page 94)

2 tsp all-purpose flour, plus more for rolling out the pizza

2 tsp coriander seeds

2 tsp nigella seeds

2 tsp dried red chili flakes

2 tsp cornmeal or semolina

¼ cup [50 g] Ghee (page 268), melted

1 cup [185 g] cherry tomatoes, halved crosswise

1 cup [160 g] grape tomatoes, halved lengthwise

1 cup [80 g] shredded mozzarella

1 Tbsp chopped fresh chives

1 Tbsp flaky sea salt, such as Maldon

Place a baking steel or pizza stone on a rack in the middle of the oven and preheat the oven to 500°F [260°C] for 30 minutes. Divide the dough into two equal parts and shape into balls. Cover one ball with a kitchen towel. On a clean, lightly floured work surface, roll the remaining ball into a circle ⅛ in [4 mm] thick and 12 in [30 cm] in diameter. Cover loosely with a kitchen towel. Repeat with the second ball of dough.

Crack the coriander lightly with a mortar and pestle, add the nigella seeds and chili flakes, and set aside.

Prepare one pizza at a time: Flip over a baking sheet, wrong-side up, and place a sheet of parchment paper on the baking sheet. Sprinkle 1 tsp of the flour and 1 tsp of the cornmeal on the parchment to coat evenly. Place a rolled-out circle of dough on top of the paper and drizzle with a little melted ghee. Spread out half of the tomatoes over the dough. Sprinkle with half the mozzarella and 1 Tbsp of the spices in the mortar. Slide the circle of dough onto the preheated baking steel, discard the parchment paper, and shut the oven door. Lower the heat to 425°F [220°C] and bake until the edges of the crust start to turn golden, 10 to 12 minutes. Garnish with half the chopped chives and flaky salt, and drizzle with a little extra ghee. Repeat with the remaining circle of dough and serve the pizzas hot.

THE APPROACH I like to pair dishes, like a Margherita pizza, with bold, unconventional flavors, like coriander and nigella seeds. Using cracked coriander seeds, rather than ground, enhances the flavor of the chili flakes. Nigella seeds pair well with tomatoes. A little sprinkle over this fresh tomato-topped pizza gives the tomatoes a fragrant, nutty flavor. You can also use olive oil instead of ghee if you prefer.

Ginger-Lentil Millet Bowl

Millet is an ancient and highly nutritious grain that needs very little water to grow. It really should become a pantry staple; it's easy to prepare and can be used in both savory and sweet preparations. In India, millet is used to make flatbreads and pilafs. This simple, one-pot meal features millet cooked with lentils and topped with strips of fried ginger and crunchy seared peanuts.

MAKES 2 SERVINGS

½ cup [110 g] pearl millet

¼ cup [50 g] red lentils, picked over for stones

1½ cups [360 ml] water

1 tsp fine sea salt

2 Tbsp extra-virgin olive oil

½ cup [70 g] finely diced red onion

2 Tbsp peanuts

One 2 in [5 cm] piece fresh ginger, peeled and cut into matchsticks

½ tsp freshly ground black pepper

1 lime, halved

6 fresh mint leaves

Rinse the millet and lentils in a fine-mesh strainer under cold running water until the runoff is no longer cloudy. Put them in a medium saucepan and add the 1½ cups [360 ml] water, ½ tsp of the salt, and 1 Tbsp of the oil. Bring to a boil over medium-high heat, and turn the heat to medium-low. Cover and simmer until both the millet and the lentils are tender, 15 to 20 minutes. Most of the water should have evaporated. Remove the saucepan from the heat and let sit, covered, for 5 minutes longer. Fluff with a fork and set aside.

In a small skillet, heat the remaining 1 Tbsp oil over medium-high heat. Add the onion and sauté until translucent, 4 to 5 minutes. Add the peanuts and cook until seared, 4 to 5 minutes more. Add the ginger and pepper and cook for an additional minute, until the ginger is lightly browned. Season with the remaining ½ tsp salt. Taste and adjust the seasonings, if necessary.

Divide the cooked lentil and millet between two bowls. Top each one with half the onion-ginger-peanut mixture. Squeeze a lime half over each bowl, garnish with the mint, and serve immediately.

THE APPROACH I cook the lentils and millet together and season them minimally with salt so their nutty flavor and texture stand out. The topping of onions, ginger, peanuts, and a squirt of fresh lime juice provides a spicy and tangy counterpoint. Frying the ginger reduces its intensity and helps flavor the oil.

Eggplant Pilaf

I love colorful, flavorful pilafs like this because it's a one-pot meal. It is made with fragrant basmati rice that's cooked with little cubes of eggplant, bright green peas, and crunchy pumpkin seeds, all coated and seasoned with spices and then finished with fresh mint. Serve it with plain yogurt, Rainbow Root Raita (page 63), or Spiced Lemon Pickle (page 274) on the side.

MAKES 4 TO 6 SERVINGS

2 cups [400 g] basmati rice

7 cups [1.8 L] water

2 lb [910 g] medium eggplants, trimmed and sliced into bite-size cubes

3 tsp fine sea salt

⅓ cup [80 ml] extra-virgin olive oil

1 medium red onion [300 g], halved and thinly sliced

1 tsp ground black pepper

1 tsp ground coriander

½ tsp dried red chili flakes

½ tsp ground turmeric

4 green cardamom pods, cracked

1 black cardamom pod, cracked

2 whole cloves

2 bay leaves

4 garlic cloves, minced

2 serrano chiles

2 Tbsp pumpkin seeds

¼ cup [60 ml] fresh lime juice

½ cup [60 g] peas, fresh or frozen

2 Tbsp chopped mint

Rinse the rice under cold running water in a fine-mesh sieve until the water no longer turns cloudy. Put the rice in a medium bowl, add 3 cups [720 ml] of the water, and let sit, covered, for about 1 hour.

Place the eggplant cubes in a large bowl and sprinkle with 1 tsp of the salt, then toss to coat. Cover the bowl with a lid or plastic wrap and allow to sit for 20 minutes. Discard any liquid that is released. Heat 2 Tbsp of the oil in a large heavy-bottomed saucepan or Dutch oven with a lid over medium-high heat. Sauté the eggplant cubes for 4 to 5 minutes, stirring occasionally, until they are tender and lightly browned. Transfer the cooked eggplant to a large bowl and keep aside until ready to use.

THE APPROACH Eggplants can have a mild bitter taste, and the bitterness can be easily removed by sprinkling the chopped vegetable with a little salt and then letting it sit for a few minutes. The salt will draw out the bitter compounds, along with some of the water. Here the cardamom pods are lightly cracked and added whole to the hot oil with the other spices. This is a milder way to perfume the rice and eggplant as they cook.

In the same saucepan, heat the remaining 3½ Tbsp oil over medium-high heat. Add the onion and cook, stirring occasionally, for 10 to 12 minutes, until they are golden brown. Then add the black pepper, coriander, red chili flakes, turmeric, green and black cardamom seeds, cloves, and bay leaves and cook for 30 to 45 seconds, until fragrant. Stir in the garlic, serrano chiles, and pumpkin seeds and cook for an additional 30 seconds. Drain the rice, stir it into the hot oil, and cook until the rice grains are completely coated with the oil and stop sticking to each other, 2 to 3 minutes. Return the cooked eggplant to the saucepan. Stir in 4 cups [960 ml] water, the lime juice, and the remaining 2 tsp salt and increase the heat to high. Bring to a rolling boil, turn the heat to medium-low, and simmer, uncovered, until most of the water has evaporated, 15 minutes. Then add the peas and cook, covered, for an additional 4 to 5 minutes, until the peas are completely tender. Remove from the heat and cover. Let sit for 5 minutes. Fluff the rice with a fork and cover again to keep warm. Garnish with the fresh mint before serving. (You can remove and discard the whole spices at this stage, but I usually prefer to leave them in.)

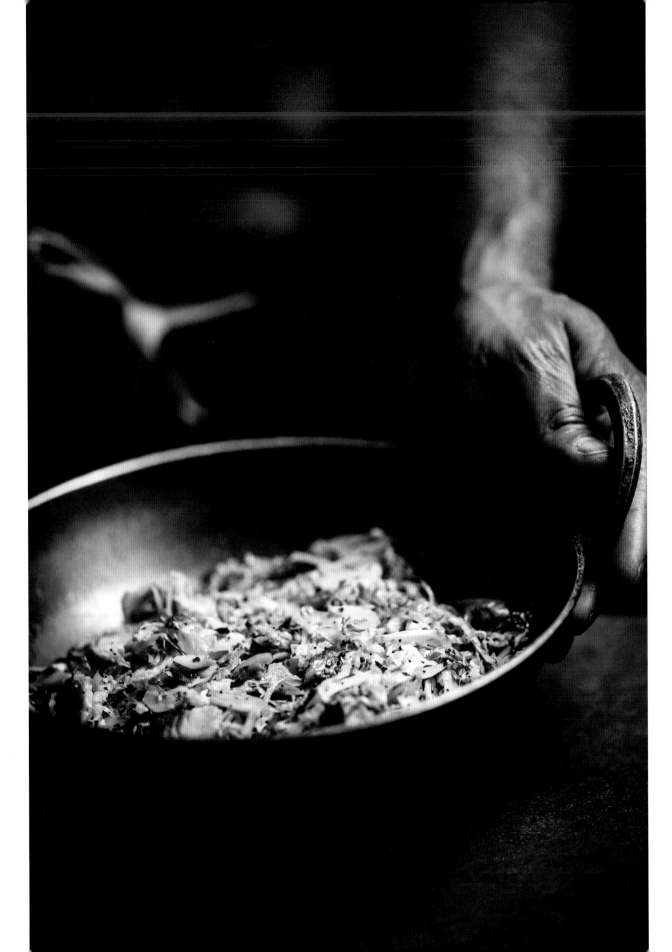

Shaved Brussels Sprouts with Poppy Seeds, Black Mustard, and Coconut Oil

We have two ridiculously tall coconut trees in the garden of our apartment complex in Bombay. They're so tall that my parents usually hire men to climb up the trees and cut off the fresh coconuts when they're ripe. The harvest is shared among neighbors, friends, and family, who put them to good use. Almost every conceivable part of the coconut is used in coastal Indian cooking. Building on that idea, I've seasoned these Brussels sprouts with a few spices tempered in hot, fragrant coconut oil to introduce a hint of that warm tropical nuttiness we associate with this fruit.

MAKES 4 SERVINGS AS A SIDE

14 oz [400 g] Brussels sprouts

1 Tbsp coconut oil

1 tsp poppy seeds

1 tsp black mustard seeds

2 Tbsp sliced raw almonds

1 tsp dried red chili flakes

2 garlic cloves, sliced

1 tsp fine sea salt

½ tsp freshly ground black pepper

1 Tbsp fresh lime juice

Trim the stems off the Brussels sprouts and remove any damaged leaves. With a mandoline, a sharp knife, or a food processor fitted with a slicing disk, cut the Brussels sprouts into thin slices.

Melt the coconut oil in a wok or a medium Dutch oven over medium-high heat. Add the poppy seeds, mustard seeds, and almonds and cook until the seeds start to sizzle and pop, 30 to 45 seconds. Add the chili flakes and garlic and cook for another 30 seconds, until the garlic is fragrant. Add the shaved Brussels sprouts and salt and pepper and stir gently to coat evenly. Turn the heat to medium-low and cook, stirring occasionally, until the Brussels sprouts start to brown and char a little, 8 to 10 minutes. Remove from the heat, add the lime juice, and taste and adjust the seasoning, if necessary. Serve hot or warm.

THE APPROACH Here hot coconut oil, with its distinctive taste and aroma, is infused with the nutty flavor of poppy seeds, the piquant flavor of black mustard seeds (don't substitute yellow ones here), and of course the heat from red chili flakes. All these different textures and flavors come together with the bittersweet burnt taste of the Brussels sprouts, which is offset by the acidity of a little fresh lime juice. If you want to kick this up a notch, add 4 to 5 fresh curry or makrut lime leaves to the hot oil when you add the chili flakes and garlic.

Charred Snap Peas and Fennel with Bacon-Guajillo Salt

If there's one thing I love about the farmers' markets in California in spring, it's the fresh snap peas. The crunchy shells hide sweet little soft peas, like pearls inside oyster shells. I like to char snap peas with fresh fennel and toss in a little bit of my Bacon-Guajillo Salt and some fresh mint leaves.

MAKES 2 TO 4 SERVINGS AS A SIDE

1 medium fennel bulb (12 oz [340 g])

1 cup [180 g] young snap peas

4 Tbsp extra-virgin olive oil

1½ tsp Bacon-Guajillo Salt (page 267)

8 to 12 fresh mint leaves

Brush the grill grate lightly with oil and preheat the grill to high. Alternatively, if using a grill pan, brush the pan with a little oil and place over medium-high heat.

Trim the bottom and stems of the fennel bulb and cut lengthwise into ¼ in [6 mm] thick slices. Put them on a baking sheet, add the snap peas, and brush the vegetables with the olive oil. Put the vegetables on the grill or into the pan and cook until nicely charred on each side.

Transfer the vegetables to a serving tray, sprinkle with the flavored salt, and scatter the mint leaves over the vegetables. Serve immediately.

THE APPROACH This is one of those dishes that is good with plain old salt and pepper, but much better when you use Bacon-Guajillo Salt, which adds heat and umami. If you don't eat bacon, try the Curry and Makrut Lime Leaf Salt (page 267) or the Nori and Yuzu Ponzu Salt (page 267). On occasion, I'll also throw in a bit of creamy fresh feta.

Roasted Young Carrots with Sesame, Chili, and Nori

Inspired by the flavors of the Japanese seasoning *shichimi togarashi*, I created this satisfying roasted carrot dish, which has become one of the most popular dishes at my supper clubs. Because these carrots are young, you really don't need to peel them before cooking, but if you must, scrape the thin skin with a paring knife, so you remove less of the carrot. You can prepare the carrots and season them the night before. Then just stick them in the oven before you're ready to serve.

MAKES 2 TO 4 SERVINGS AS A SIDE

1 lb [455 g] small young carrots

1 Tbsp chopped nori

1 Tbsp black sesame seeds

1 tsp white sesame seeds

1 tsp caraway seeds

1 tsp dried red chili flakes

1 tsp flaky sea salt, such as Maldon

2 Tbsp extra-virgin olive oil

Preheat the oven to 425°F [220°C]. Trim the tops of the carrots. Pull off any tiny roots that may be attached to the carrots and transfer the carrots to a baking sheet or roasting pan. Sprinkle the nori, sesame seeds, caraway, chili flakes, and salt over the carrots and drizzle with the olive oil. Roast the carrots, flipping occasionally, until they're slightly charred and crispy on the ends, 25 to 30 minutes. Serve hot or warm.

THE APPROACH Carrots are sensational roasted because when charred, they become bittersweet. When I make my *shichimi togarashi*–inspired spice mixture, I don't grind the whole seeds because, left whole, they add both flavor and visual appeal. Every bite is a little different, because the seeds create random hot spots throughout the dish.

Fingerlings with Crispy Sage and Garlicky Kefir Crème Fraîche

I am a very big fan of potatoes. This recipe requires minimal fuss and delivers a satisfying contrast between textures, flavors, and even temperatures.

MAKES 4 SERVINGS AS A SIDE

8 garlic cloves

2 tsp extra-virgin olive oil

1½ lb [680 g] fingerling potatoes

1½ tsp fine sea salt

2 tsp dried red chili flakes

6 to 8 fresh sage leaves

½ tsp freshly ground black pepper

1 cup [200 g] Kefir Crème Fraîche (page 260)
    or store-bought crème fraîche

1 Tbsp thinly sliced fresh chives

Preheat the oven to 425°F [220°C]. Drizzle the garlic cloves with 1 tsp of the olive oil and wrap in aluminum foil. Roast until tender, 25 to 30 minutes. Remove from the oven and let cool in the foil to room temperature. Leave the oven on.

Halve the potatoes lengthwise and put in a medium bowl. Add the remaining 1 tsp olive oil, 1 tsp of the salt, the chili flakes, the sage leaves, and the black pepper. Toss to coat evenly. Transfer to a medium roasting pan and roast for about 15 minutes. Turn over the potatoes and continue roasting until the potatoes are golden brown and slightly charred and the sage leaves are slightly crisp, about 15 minutes more. Remove from the oven.

While the potatoes are cooking, prepare the sauce: Peel the cooled garlic cloves and smash to a smooth paste with the side of a knife. Transfer to a small bowl and add the crème fraîche and the remaining ½ tsp salt. Stir with a fork to combine. Taste and adjust the seasoning, if necessary, and transfer to a serving bowl.

Garnish the potatoes with the chives and serve hot, with the sauce on the side.

THE APPROACH The red chili flakes coat the potatoes with a little heat, the sage provides aroma and crunch, and the crème fraîche cools everything off.

CHAPTER 4: Seafood

Because I grew up on the coast, my family ate more fish than meat. My grandmother was Catholic and would always have fish or shrimp at the table on Friday. Usually we'd eat seafood cooked in a spicy broth or a stew made with freshly grated coconut or green unripe mango, with rice or bread on the side. We also enjoyed fried oysters and scallops and dried fish and shrimp pickled with chiles and turmeric.

When I moved to the United States, I was exposed to a whole new world, where raw oysters, ceviche, crudo, gravlax, and fried catfish were celebrated with fervor. Over time, I learned to recognize and appreciate regional differences in cooking methods and flavor for each type of seafood, and I loved it all.

Fish cooks quickly, thanks to its small muscle fibers, so it's important to watch it carefully. You can create exciting flavor profiles by experimenting with acids such as vinegar, fresh mangoes, verjus, tamarind, and white wine. (Don't use red wine, because the tannins react with natural fish oils and create an unpleasant taste and smell.) For the fat, try Ghee (page 268) and mustard oil.

Oysters with Passion Fruit Mignonette

Passion fruit is used most often to make desserts, but it's also great in seafood dishes. Its heavenly aroma permeates this sweet-and-sour mignonette, which makes a delightful counterpoint to briny raw oysters. You will find passion fruit juice at greengrocers and Mexican and Asian markets, where it's often frozen. Look for large, meaty oysters like Kumamoto, Miyagi, and Blue Point.

MAKES 6 APPETIZER SERVINGS

¼ cup [60 ml] passion fruit juice (from about 3 passion fruits)

¼ cup [60 ml] rice wine vinegar

1 tsp sugar

¼ tsp fine sea salt

¼ tsp freshly ground black pepper

2 shallots, minced

2 tsp minced chives

1 tsp dried red chili flakes

24 freshly shucked oysters on the half shell (see page 42)

In a small bowl, stir together the passion fruit juice, rice wine vinegar, sugar, salt, and pepper. Stir in the shallots, chives, and red chili flakes. Taste and adjust the sweetness and seasoning, if necessary.

To serve, place the oysters in a serving dish filled with ice. Drizzle the oysters with the mignonette.

THE APPROACH The passion fruit in the mignonette sauce adds a sweet, tropical note, while complementing the sour taste of the vinegar and the heat of the chili flakes. The juice of other acidic fruits, such as fresh pineapple, can be substituted. Just remember to taste and adjust the acidity or sweetness of the mignonette as needed.

Turmeric and Lime Mussel Broth

I first tasted makrut lime leaves in Bombay when I went to my friend Praphat's home for dinner. Praphat's mother, Sriwan, who is from Thailand, cooked us an elaborate meal made with fresh herbs and spices and the leaves of a makrut lime tree, which grew in her backyard. She would pluck the fresh leaves off her tree and toss them into hot oil, which she used to start a soup. Taking a page out of Sriwan's book, I add makrut leaves to ghee, after infusing it with turmeric and ginger. Serve with a slice or two of buttered and toasted baguette. You can find makrut lime leaves (formerly known as kaffir) in most Asian markets and in the international aisles of some grocery stores. This broth also works great with clams.

MAKES 2 SERVINGS

2 lb [910 g] mussels

1 Tbsp Ghee (page 268) or My Nit'r Qibe (page 270)

1 cup [135 g] minced shallots

1 tsp garam masala, homemade (page 263) or store-bought

One 2 in [5 cm] piece fresh turmeric root, peeled and cut into matchsticks

4 makrut lime leaves, preferably fresh

1 whole Kashmiri chile

1 Tbsp tomato paste

One 2 in [5 cm] piece fresh ginger, peeled and cut into matchsticks

1 tsp kosher salt

One 13½ oz [400 ml] can coconut milk

¼ cup [60 ml] fresh lime juice

2 Tbsp thinly sliced scallion (white and green parts)

Rinse the mussels under cold running water, scrubbing well to remove any grit. Keep on ice in the refrigerator while building the broth.

In a heavy medium stockpot, heat the ghee over medium-high heat. Sauté the shallots until translucent, 4 to 5 minutes. Add the garam masala and turmeric root and cook for 1 more minute. Add the lime leaves and Kashmiri chile and cook until fragrant, 30 seconds. Stir in the tomato paste and ginger and cook for 2 minutes, stirring constantly. Stir in the salt and the coconut milk, and then gently stir in the mussels. Cover the stockpot and cook until the mussels open, 12 to 15 minutes. Discard any unopened mussels. Stir in the lime juice and taste and add more salt, if necessary. Garnish the broth with the scallions and serve immediately.

THE APPROACH In this broth, the fresh turmeric root adds a beautiful golden color while the fresh ginger adds spiciness and texture. Both of them possess starch, which helps thicken the broth as it is heated. To maximize the impact of the aromatic ingredients, I heat them in a flavorful fat, such as ghee or the Ethiopian spiced butter *nit'r qibe*. The coconut milk and mussels absorb these flavors as they cook. The addition of lime leaves and juice brightens the broth and counterbalances the heat.

Sumac-Seared Scallops with Mostarda

I spent four wonderful summers celebrating the Fourth of July at the Pines on Fire Island, in New York. Michael and I would share a house with some of our closest friends and spend a week on that little oasis. There was only one grocery store near us, and one evening, I ended up with a bunch of scallops but no lemon or lime juice with which to flavor them. Thankfully, sumac came to my rescue and no one noticed the absence of fresh citrus at dinner. Serve these scallops hot over my Apple and Pear Mostarda (page 281).

MAKES 3 TO 4 APPETIZER SERVINGS

12 sea scallops

½ tsp fine sea salt

½ tsp freshly ground black pepper

1 tsp ground sumac

3 to 4 Tbsp Ghee (page 268)

1 cup [250 g] Apple and Pear Mostarda (page 281)

1 Tbsp water (optional)

2 Tbsp thinly sliced fresh cilantro or flat-leaf parsley leaves (optional)

Pat the scallops dry with paper towels. Mix the salt, pepper, and sumac in a small bowl and sprinkle all over the scallops to season.

In a medium skillet, preferably cast-iron, heat the ghee over high heat. When the skillet is hot and the ghee starts to smoke, add the scallops. Cook until they develop a deep golden brown crust, 1½ to 2 minutes per side. Drain the scallops on paper towels.

In a small saucepan, heat the mostarda over medium-low heat until it just starts to simmer, 2 to 3 minutes (do not let it boil). If the mostarda seems too thick, stir in the water. Spread out the mostarda on a serving dish and arrange the hot scallops on top. Garnish with the cilantro and serve immediately.

THE APPROACH Most seafood benefits from a dash of acid. In this recipe, however, I skip the usual suspects (lemons, limes, and vinegar) and opt for sumac, a common spice in North African and Middle Eastern households. The small fruit, from which the powdered sumac is obtained, has a strong, lemony acidity, which makes sumac a great substitute when you're out of citrus.

I recommend searing the scallops in ghee because of its nutty caramel notes, but you can use duck fat if you prefer a more baconlike flavor. When prepping the scallops, blot them with paper towels so they're as dry as possible to ensure a nice, dark sear. I love to serve these scallops with something fruity, and the Apple and Pear Mostarda provides that extra special dash of flavor.

Grilled Grape Leaf–Wrapped Shrimp

In India, fresh banana and turmeric leaves are traditionally used to wrap fish and shrimp before they're cooked on hot grills. This technique, which actually steams the fish, imbues it with flavor and makes for a dramatic presentation. Since it's hard to find fresh banana and turmeric leaves in America (try Asian markets), I use brined grape leaves here instead. Serve these little parcels with rice pilaf (page 256) or Naan (page 94). If you can't find raw pistachios, unsalted roasted pistachios will work.

MAKES 7 SERVINGS

¼ cup [60 ml] extra-virgin olive oil

½ cup [70 g] unsalted pistachios, preferably raw

2 Tbsp water

2 serrano chiles, seeded if desired

1 stalk lemongrass (white part only)

1 bunch (1½ oz [40 g]) fresh cilantro

1 cup (¾ oz [20 g]) packed baby arugula

8 black peppercorns

1 tsp fine sea salt

Juice of 1 lemon

14 large shrimp, peeled and deveined

14 brined grape leaves, unfolded and drained

Vegetable oil for brushing the grape leaf packages

In a blender, combine the olive oil, pistachios, water, serrano chiles, lemongrass, cilantro, arugula, peppercorns, salt, and lemon juice. Pulse on high speed for a few seconds, until you get a coarse paste. Taste and adjust the seasoning, if necessary. Transfer half to a large bowl and the rest to a serving dish.

Add the shrimp to the large bowl containing the pistachio and lemongrass mixture. Toss to coat evenly, cover, and refrigerate for 1 hour.

Meanwhile, brush the grill grate lightly with oil and preheat the grill to high. Soak seven bamboo skewers in water for 30 minutes.

Remove the shrimp from the refrigerator. Lay a grape leaf flat on a clean work surface, shiny-side down. Place one piece of marinated shrimp in the center with a little marinade. Fold the ends of the leaf over the shrimp and then roll it over itself to form a little parcel. Insert a bamboo skewer to hold the envelope together. Brush the surface of the grape leaf with a little oil.

THE APPROACH Shrimp comes to life when paired with fresh herbs and citrus. The pistachio and lemongrass mixture, with its fiery serrano chiles, adds heat and a creamy texture. While the shrimp cook inside their grape leaf envelopes, they soak up all the flavors in the marinade. The result is tender yet flavorful shrimp.

Repeat with the remaining shrimp and grape leaves, placing two parcels on each skewer. Grill the shrimp envelopes for 3 to 4 minutes on each side, brushing with oil if the leaves stick to the grate or become dry. Remove from the grill and serve hot with the reserved pistachio and lemongrass mixture on the side.

Crab Cakes with Lemongrass and Green Mango

My mom loved crab cakes so much she'd sometimes lose count as she made batch after batch. I'd take advantage of the abundance and sneak one away every time I walked through the kitchen. She never said a word, but she must have known what was going on. What makes these crab cakes stand out is the combination of hot and sour flavors from the minced Thai chiles and bits of fresh green mango. I usually use equal parts lump and back fin.

MAKES 7 APPETIZER SERVINGS

1 lb [455 g] fresh crabmeat

4 shallots, minced

2 Tbsp minced lemongrass (white part only)

3 Tbsp finely diced fresh green mango

2 Tbsp fresh cilantro leaves

2 Thai chiles, seeded, if desired, and minced

1 Tbsp Dijon mustard

1 tsp coriander seeds

1 tsp garam masala, homemade (page 263) or store-bought

1 whole lime, plus 2 limes, cut into wedges (optional)

½ tsp fine sea salt

¼ cup [35 g] dry bread crumbs

2 large egg yolks

Vegetable oil for frying

Sweet and Smoky Tahini Sauce (page 278) or Charred Green Garlic and Yuzu Ponzu Sauce (page 277), for serving (optional)

In a large bowl, combine the crabmeat, shallots, lemongrass, mango, cilantro, Thai chiles, and mustard. Using a mortar and pestle or spice grinder, grind the coriander seeds to a coarse powder and add to the crabmeat with the garam masala. Grate the lime zest and juice the whole lime. Add 1 tsp of the zest and 1 Tbsp of the juice to the crabmeat, discarding the remaining zest and juice. Add the salt and bread crumbs and mix gently to combine. Add the egg yolks and fold it into the crabmeat mixture. Divide the mixture into fourteen equal parts and shape into 2 in [5 cm] rounds, 1 in [2.5 cm] thick.

Heat 1 to 1½ Tbsp of oil in a medium cast-iron or nonstick skillet over medium-low heat. Place four cakes in the skillet and cook until golden brown and crispy, 2½ to 3 minutes on each side. Drain on paper towels. Transfer to a plate and serve with the lime wedges and sauce, if desired.

THE APPROACH In the early months of summer, young green mangoes start showing up at the markets in India. These unripe mangoes have a distinctly sour, fruity taste and their flesh is tender, yet firm. Green mangoes are often used in Goan cuisine, especially with seafood. Fresh mango works very well with hot chiles, while the lemongrass, lime, and coriander brighten the flavors of the crab cakes even more.

Ginger-Garlic Stir-Fried Crab

I've eaten blue crabs in Maryland, Dungeness crabs in San Francisco, and mud crabs in Bombay, and I've noticed that no matter which coast you're on or in which country, locals love to celebrate crab season. I like my crabs cracked gently so it's easy to access the juicy, tender meat hidden inside. They're especially good stir-fried and coated with this highly aromatic sauce made with ginger, garlic, chiles, and, of course, a little bit of lime juice.

MAKES 2 SERVINGS

2 tsp fine sea salt

4 lb [1.8 kg] live crabs

¼ cup [60 ml] vegetable oil

1 cup [140 g] finely diced red onion

1 tsp ground coriander

¼ cup [35 g] minced garlic

¼ cup [25 g] grated peeled fresh ginger

2 serrano chiles, seeded, if desired, and minced

½ tsp freshly ground black pepper

1 tsp jaggery or brown sugar

Juice of 1 lime

2 Tbsp chopped fresh cilantro

Cooked rice, pilaf (page 256), or bread, such as Naan (page 94), for serving

Fill a large bowl with ice and plenty of cool water. Set aside until this ice bath is needed.

Fill a large stockpot with water, add 1 tsp of the salt, and bring to a rolling boil over high heat. Drop in the crabs and cook until the shells turn orange, about 10 minutes. Remove with a slotted spoon or a pair of tongs and transfer to the ice bath. Once the crabs are cool and easy to handle, drain the ice bath. To partially remove the shell from each crab, discard the top shell, the white spongy gills, the greenish-brown liver, and the mouthparts. If you like, you can leave the soft, yellow fat in the crab for a richer taste. Flip over the crab and, using a cleaver or large kitchen knife, cut the crab in half lengthwise along its midline. Using a mallet, lightly crack the shell.

Continued

THE APPROACH Cooking this dish over high heat releases the aromas and flavors of the spices, onions, garlic, and ginger. It also promotes caramelization, which adds bitter-sweet flavors.

Heat a large Dutch oven, stockpot, or wok over high heat, and add the oil. When the oil is hot, add the onion and sauté until translucent, 4 to 5 minutes. Add the coriander, garlic, ginger, and chiles and cook until fragrant, 30 to 45 seconds. Add the crabs, pepper, jaggery, and remaining 1 tsp salt. Stir gently to coat the crabs with the aromatics and turn the heat to low. Cover and cook, stirring occasionally, until most of the liquid has evaporated from the pot and the oil has separated from the onion mixture, 12 to 15 minutes. Remove from the heat. Drizzle the lime juice over the crabs and garnish with the fresh cilantro. Serve hot with the rice, pilaf, or bread.

Tandoori Swordfish Steaks

Swordfish steaks take exceptionally well to marinades, especially this one. While the number of spices in the yogurt marinade may appear daunting, you probably have most of them in your pantry. The Pumpkin-Garlic Purée served on the side gets a drizzle of hot coconut oil infused with serrano chiles and whole spices. For a deep red cast to the fish, grind 2 to 3 Tbsp of chopped cooked red beets into the yogurt and proceed as directed.

MAKES 2 SERVINGS

Pumpkin-Garlic Purée

1 small pumpkin (about 1½ lb [680 g])

2 Tbsp extra-virgin olive oil

8 garlic cloves, sliced

4 black peppercorns

½ cup [120 ml] water

1 tsp fine sea salt

Swordfish Steaks

2 Tbsp plain Greek yogurt

1 Tbsp fresh lemon juice

2 garlic cloves, chopped

2 whole cloves

Seeds from 1 green cardamom pod, crushed

1 tsp fine sea salt

One ½ in [12 mm] piece fresh ginger, peeled and chopped

½ tsp ground turmeric

½ tsp coriander seeds

½ tsp ground Kashmiri chile

½ tsp paprika

½ tsp freshly ground black pepper

Two 1 in [2.5 cm] thick swordfish steaks (about 8 oz [230 g] each)

2 Tbsp vegetable oil, plus more for grilling

Continued

THE APPROACH Because it's acidic, yogurt is good for marinating the fish, while the spices add flavor and aroma. I don't toast the whole spices before using in the marinade because they cook later on the hot grill, and toasting them too early would weaken their potency. The best way to bring a pop of flavor to mild foods like pumpkins, or even potatoes, is to infuse hot oil with spices and then drizzle the spiced oil on top, as I've done here.

Coconut Oil Drizzle

2 Tbsp coconut oil

1 tsp nigella seeds

1 tsp cumin seeds

1 tsp coriander seeds

2 serrano chiles, halved lengthwise

Flaky sea salt, such as Maldon

To make the pumpkin purée: Preheat the oven to 425°F [220°C]. Trim the stem and cut the pumpkin in half through the equator. Use a large spoon to scrape out the seeds. Place the pumpkin halves on a baking sheet, flesh-side up, and brush with the olive oil. Sprinkle with the garlic and peppercorns. Roast until tender, 35 to 40 minutes. Remove from the oven and let cool for 8 to 10 minutes. Scrape the pulp out of the shells, discarding the shells. Transfer the pulp (along with the garlic and peppercorns) to a blender or food processor. Add the water and salt and blend to a smooth purée. Taste and adjust the seasoning, if necessary. Transfer to a serving bowl or platter and keep warm.

To make the swordfish: While the pumpkin is roasting, in a clean blender, combine everything but the fish and the oil. Blend until smooth. Pat the fish steaks dry with paper towels and place on a large plate. Rub the marinade on both sides and cover with plastic wrap. Refrigerate for 1 hour. Brush the grates of a grill lightly with oil and preheat the grill to high. Drizzle 1½ tsp of the oil on each side of each fish and place on the hot grill. Cook on one side until it comes off the grates easily, 4 to 5 minutes. (Resist the urge to move it around too much, or it will rip.) Flip the fish over and cook until firm to the touch, another 4 to 5 minutes. Or, if using a grill pan, heat the pan over high heat, coat lightly with oil, and cook the fish. Transfer the grilled fish steaks to the serving dish with the prepared pumpkin.

To make the drizzle: Melt the coconut oil in a small saucepan over medium-high heat. Add the nigella seeds, cumin seeds, coriander seeds, and serrano chiles and cook until fragrant, 30 to 45 seconds. Pour the drizzle over the pumpkin purée, sprinkle with a little flaky salt, and serve immediately.

Turmeric-and-Chile-Roasted Red Snapper with Melon Salsa

In Western countries, fish is often stuffed with slices of lemon and then grilled. In the coastal territory of Goa, vinegar is the more common acid of choice. Goan vinegar is usually obtained from toddy, the sap of the coconut palm, which is left to ferment. This fish dish doesn't require much work, but the payoff is big.

MAKES 2 SERVINGS

Corn and Cantaloupe Salsa

2 cups [270 g] fresh yellow corn kernels

2 cups [270 g] diced ripe cantaloupe

2 Tbsp finely minced shallot

2 Tbsp fresh cilantro leaves

1 serrano chile, seeded, if desired, and minced

2 Tbsp fresh lime juice

½ tsp *kala namak* (Indian black salt) or fine sea salt

Red Snapper

2 Tbsp coconut vinegar or cider vinegar

1 tsp ground turmeric

1 tsp cayenne pepper

1 tsp fine sea salt

One 2 lb [910 g] whole red snapper, cleaned and scaled

2 Tbsp extra-virgin olive oil

1 lime, quartered

To make the salsa: Fill a medium pot with water and bring to a boil over high heat. Add the corn and boil until tender, 3 to 4 minutes. Drain and transfer the corn to a large bowl. Add the cantaloupe, shallots, cilantro, serrano chile, lime juice, and black salt. Taste and adjust the seasoning, if necessary. Cover the bowl and refrigerate for at least 30 minutes.

To make the fish: Preheat the oven to 375°F [190°C]. In a small bowl, mix together the vinegar, turmeric, cayenne, and salt and set aside. Run a sharp paring knife along the dorsal (upper) side of the fish to create a deep pocket between the flesh and the spine, starting about 1 in [2.5 cm] from the tail and stopping about 1 in [2.5 cm] before you reach the head.

THE APPROACH When I season a whole fish before cooking, I want the flesh to come into contact with the spices and absorb them. Instead of putting the spice mixture in the body cavity, which is the most common method, I make a slit on top, across the length of the fish. This exposes the flesh, allowing the spices to penetrate more easily. Because the fish is seasoned with ground chile and served hot, I balance both types of heat with a cool, fruity salsa. The combination of sweet corn and cantaloupe, lime juice, and salty *kala namak* makes for a light and refreshing meal.

Place in a baking dish. Spread the vinegar-spice mixture inside the pocket on both sides of the fish. Cover tightly with plastic wrap and refrigerate for 30 minutes.

Brush both sides of the skin with the olive oil. Roast for 10 to 15 minutes, or until the skin is crisp and the flesh is opaque white and flakes easily. Serve hot or warm with the salsa and lime wedges on the side.

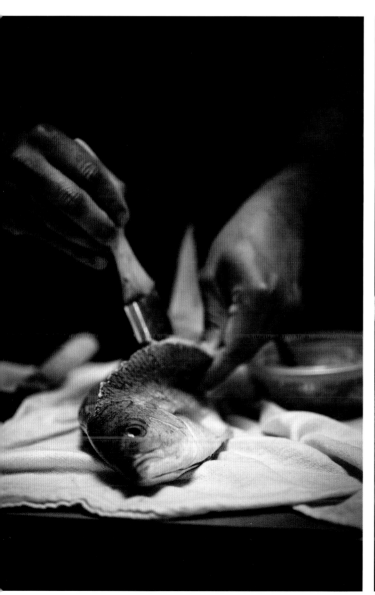

Coriander Gravlax

Ever since I first learned to prepare gravlax from Diana Henry's cookbook *Salt Sugar Smoke*, I've been fascinated by the process of curing fish with salt. The results are quite astounding. Here, most of the moisture from the fatty salmon is drawn out by the salt and sugar, while the flesh absorbs the flavors of the spices. You may substitute Lapsang Souchong tea leaves for the Darjeeling if you prefer a smoky flavor and deeper notes of umami. I place thin slices of this gravlax on bagels or toasted sourdough bread with a dab of Hot Green Chutney (page 277) or Sweet and Smoky Tahini Sauce (page 278) and thinly sliced shallots or red onions.

MAKES 4 TO 6 SERVINGS (1 LB [455 G] SALMON)

2½ Tbsp Darjeeling tea leaves

1 Tbsp black peppercorns

1 Tbsp coriander seeds

3 oz [85 g] Himalayan pink salt (coarse grains)

1 Tbsp sugar

Zest of 1 lemon

1 lb [455 g] sashimi-grade salmon fillets with skin

1 Tbsp Pernod or plain vodka

Prepare the curing mixture by using a mortar and pestle or a spice grinder to grind the tea leaves, peppercorns, and coriander to a coarse powder. Transfer to a small bowl and add the pink salt, sugar, and lemon zest and stir to combine.

Pat the salmon dry with paper towels. Remove any pin bones or scales from the fish. Cut a sheet of aluminum foil large enough to wrap the entire piece of salmon. Place the salmon, skin-side down, in the center of the foil and brush with the Pernod. Sprinkle the curing mixture over the fish, making sure the entire fish is completely coated. Wrap the fish tightly with the foil and put on a plate or in a baking dish. Weight the wrapped fish with a heavy can and refrigerate for 36 to 48 hours, turning the fish periodically to redistribute the curing mixture. The fish will be slightly firm to the touch when cured. Unwrap the foil, scrape the curing mixture off the salmon, and discard any accumulated juices. If you prefer a less briny flavor, rinse the fish with cold filtered water and pat dry.

To serve, use a sharp knife to thinly slice the gravlax against the grain at a 45-degree angle, and transfer the fish to a serving plate. The cured fish should keep for a few days in the refrigerator, but discard it as soon as you notice an off odor.

THE APPROACH Gravlax is prepared by lightly curing oily fish like salmon with a mixture of salt and sugar to draw out its moisture. Essential oils from the peppercorns, coriander, and lemon infuse the fish as it cures, making this gravlax especially flavorful and aromatic.

CHAPTER 5: **Eggs + Poultry**

There are so many ways to flavor eggs. I love boiled eggs at breakfast with flaky salt and black pepper, but sometimes I prefer to season them with a few pinches of za'atar (page 264) or toasted ground cumin and coriander. These spices shine against a warm, runny yolk. Or I'll add a few crispy cubes of fried pancetta to soft-boiled eggs, still cozy in their shells. On other mornings, I'll load my hard-boiled eggs with generous spoonfuls of green chutney (page 277) and a few drops of a good olive oil and nibble buttered toast on the side.

Like eggs, chicken and turkey are extremely versatile. I grew up eating a lot of chicken, but turkey was new to me when I moved to America. I soon learned that despite their differences in size and flavor, it's easy to adapt a recipe for one to fit the other. In fact, most of the recipes in this chapter will suit chicken and turkey equally well. A piece of grilled chicken or turkey at lunch can be so much more. Drizzle it with a little chile oil or toasted sesame oil or add some lemon pickle (page 274) before sandwiching it between thick slices of toasted bread.

Keep the skin on your birds when you can. It's rich in fat and therefore adds flavor. It also helps protect the meat as it cooks, and as we all know, when skin crisps up, the texture is fantastic (think fried chicken or chicken wings). In some parts of India, the skin of fowl is traditionally thought to be unclean, so you'll notice that several marinades (especially those that are yogurt- or citrus-based) are designed to penetrate the tissue directly.

Finally, I prefer to cook chicken and turkey with the bone in whenever possible. It improves flavor, retains moisture, and avoids the rather sterile impression a boneless cut often leaves.

I try to be mindful when sourcing poultry and eggs and encourage you to do the same. When you shop, try to find out how the chickens are housed, the kind of food they are fed, and the number of hours they roam around the farm. The more you know, the better you are as a consumer and as a cook!

Bombay Frittata

Almost every Sunday my mom would serve us slices of hot buttered toast, warm cups of chai, and omelets or scrambled eggs seasoned with garam masala. Now I like to flavor my frittatas with garam masala, along with turmeric and chili flakes. Chopped bits of crisp bacon or sautéed leeks make nice add-ins.

MAKES 6 SERVINGS

12 large eggs

½ cup [100 g] Kefir Crème Fraîche (page 260) or store-bought crème fraîche

½ cup [70 g] finely chopped red onion

2 scallions, thinly sliced (white and green parts)

2 garlic cloves, thinly sliced

4 Tbsp fresh cilantro leaves

½ tsp garam masala, homemade (page 263) or store-bought

½ tsp fine sea salt

½ tsp freshly ground black pepper

½ tsp ground turmeric

¼ tsp dried red chili flakes

2 Tbsp Ghee (page 268) or vegetable oil

¼ cup [30 g] crumbled Paneer (page 260) or feta

Position a rack in the upper third of the oven and preheat the oven to 350°F [180°C].

In a large bowl, combine the eggs, crème fraîche, onion, scallions, garlic, cilantro, garam masala, salt, pepper, turmeric, and chili flakes and beat with a whisk or fork; do not overbeat.

Heat the ghee in a 12 in [30.5 cm] ovenproof skillet, such as cast iron, over medium-high heat, tilting the skillet to coat evenly with the fat. When the ghee bubbles, pour the eggs into the center of the skillet, shaking to distribute evenly. Cook, undisturbed, until the frittata starts to firm up on the bottom and along the sides but is still slightly jiggly on top, about 5 minutes. Sprinkle with the paneer and transfer the skillet to the oven. Cook until golden brown, 20 to 25 minutes. Serve warm.

THE APPROACH I don't sauté the onions and aromatics before adding them to the eggs because I want them to retain their sharp bite. Ghee is my fat of choice because it adds a rich, nutty aroma that complements the garam masala.

Baked Eggs with Artichoke Hearts

Baked eggs are a visual delight and more versatile than you might think. They're a perfect topper for an endless array of savory dishes, like this breakfast-meets-dinner offering. The eggs sit on top of a fragrant combination of artichoke hearts and bread, and it all bakes at the same time. It's an easy midweek meal with a big payoff.

MAKES 2 TO 4 SERVINGS

2 Tbsp Ghee (page 268), melted, plus extra to grease the pan

6 black peppercorns

2 whole cloves

¼ tsp fenugreek seeds

⅛ tsp ground nutmeg

One 14 oz [400 g] can quartered artichoke hearts packed in water, drained

2 cups [60 g] cubed stale crusty bread, such as sourdough (½ inch [12 mm] cubes)

1 cup [80 g] grated mozzarella

4 garlic cloves, minced

2 Tbsp minced shallot

2 Tbsp fresh lemon juice

1 Tbsp minced fresh chives

1 serrano chile, seeded, if desired, and minced

½ tsp fine sea salt

4 large eggs

Preheat the oven to 375°F [190°C]. Grease a 9 in [23 cm] round cake or pie pan with ghee.

With a mortar and pestle or spice grinder, grind the peppercorns, cloves, and fenugreek to a fine powder. Transfer to a large bowl and add the nutmeg, 2 Tbsp ghee, artichoke hearts, bread cubes, mozzarella, garlic, shallots, lemon juice, chives, serrano chile, and salt. Cover and let sit at room temperature for 30 minutes.

Spread out the bread-artichoke mixture in the pan. Crack the eggs over the top and place the pan in the oven. Bake until the bread turns golden brown and the eggs are cooked to your liking, 16 to 18 minutes. (You may need to add a few extra minutes for hard-cooked eggs.) Serve hot.

THE APPROACH This simple and humble dish is extremely flavorful. The 30-minute rest before you add the eggs is critical, as it allows the bread to fully absorb all the seasonings. The cloves, fenugreek, nutmeg, garlic, and ghee all lend complex notes, while the lemon juice brightens the flavors and cuts through the richness.

Egg Salad with Toasted Coriander

If you asked me what I love to pack for lunch on picnics and trips, I'd tell you egg salad sandwiches and bottles of ice-cold lemonade. This is my grown-up version of egg salad—not too creamy, and with a little heat from the Thai chile and the hot sauce.

MAKES 4 SERVINGS (2½ CUPS [450 G] EGG SALAD)

1 Tbsp coriander seeds

6 Hard-Boiled Eggs (page 255), peeled and coarsely chopped

¼ cup [60 g] mayonnaise

4 roasted garlic cloves (page 259), smashed

1 Thai chile, seeded and minced

2 Tbsp minced fresh chives

1 Tbsp drained capers

1 tsp fine sea salt

½ tsp freshly ground black pepper

1 Tbsp hot sauce (optional)

8 thick slices whole-grain bread

Heat a small skillet over medium-high heat. Add the coriander seeds and toast until fragrant, swirling the seeds occasionally so they toast evenly, 30 to 45 seconds. Transfer to a mortar and pestle or spice grinder and grind to a coarse powder.

Put the ground coriander in a medium bowl and add the eggs, mayonnaise, garlic, chile, chives, capers, salt, pepper, and hot sauce (if using). Mash with a potato masher and stir to combine. Taste and adjust the seasoning, if necessary.

Divide the egg salad among four slices of bread, spreading it out to cover. Top each one with another slice of bread, cut in half if you like, and serve.

THE APPROACH This egg salad includes the briny essence of capers and a little hot sauce to balance the creamy texture of the eggs and mayonnaise. But it's the smokiness of the ground toasted coriander seeds that makes the egg salad extra special. When toasted, coriander seeds acquire a slightly smoky taste that bumps up the flavor profile of this salad.

Deviled Eggs with Creamy Tahini and Za'atar

Ever since I married a Southerner, I've made more deviled eggs than I care to count. But there's always one rule: Michael must boil and peel the eggs, and I'll do the rest. This way it's teamwork! Deviled eggs might look dainty and maybe even tricky, but they are very forgiving. You can be as fussy as you want and pipe the filling with a fancy pastry tip, or go rogue and use a spoon. This recipe was inspired by Michael's love for all things eggs and hummus. I like to garnish the eggs with mustard greens, which have a bite to them that reminds me of horseradish. You can find them in most Asian grocery stores and at farmers' markets.

MAKES 4 TO 6 SERVINGS (12 DEVILED EGGS)

6 Hard-Boiled Eggs (page 255)

¼ cup [60 g] plain full-fat Greek yogurt

¼ cup [60 ml] walnut oil or extra-virgin olive oil

2 Tbsp tahini

1 Tbsp fresh lemon juice

1 tsp za'atar, homemade (page 264) or store-bought

½ tsp fine sea salt

½ tsp ground white pepper

1 Tbsp minced fresh chives

12 leaves baby mustard greens

Peel the eggs and halve lengthwise with a sharp knife. Using a teaspoon, carefully pop out the yolks and put in a large bowl. Add the yogurt, walnut oil, tahini, lemon juice, za'atar, salt, and pepper. Whisk the ingredients until creamy, light, and smooth (no lumps!), 3 to 4 minutes. Taste and adjust the seasoning, if necessary.

Transfer the yolk mixture to a pastry bag fitted with a large star tip. Pipe into the cavities of the egg white halves. Garnish with the fresh chives and mustard leaves. Deviled eggs are best eaten the day they're made.

THE APPROACH The rich, creamy filling is offset by the acidity of the yogurt, lemon juice, and sumac, and the brightness of the za'atar. The eggs get a peppery bite from the mustard leaves.

Hot Green Chutney–Roasted Chicken

Roasting chickens during pockets of spare time on the weekends pays huge dividends during busy weeks. A whole chicken can feed a lot of people, and for a family of two like ours, it lasts a few days. Plus, a roasted chicken can be repurposed for an endless number of dishes, including salad (page 148), sandwiches, mac and cheese . . . the possibilities are endless. In this nifty roast chicken, I lace the meat with green chutney and serve extra on the side for dunking.

MAKES 6 SERVINGS

One 5 lb [2.3 kg] whole roasting chicken

1½ cups [375 g] Hot Green Chutney (page 277)

Kosher salt

2 cups [480 ml] low-sodium chicken broth

Put the chicken in a large roasting pan or baking dish. Pat the chicken dry with paper towels. Slip your fingers between the skin and flesh to loosen the skin. Massage ½ cup [125 g] of the chutney all over the meat, spreading to coat as evenly as possible. Rub generously with salt over the skin. Cover the pan with plastic wrap and refrigerate for at least 2 hours, and preferably overnight.

Position a rack in the lower third of the oven and preheat the oven to 400°F [200°C]. Unwrap the chicken and pour the broth into the pan. Roast the chicken for at least 2 hours, basting it with the broth every 15 to 20 minutes, until the internal temperature registers 165°F [74°C] on an instant-read thermometer and the skin turns golden brown. Remove from the oven and transfer the chicken to a serving platter. Tent loosely with foil and let sit for 10 minutes. (Collect any liquid left behind in the pan and cover and refrigerate or freeze for future use, such as soup.)

Serve the chicken warm with the remaining 1 cup [250 g] green chutney on the side for a dipping sauce.

THE APPROACH You can flavor a whole chicken with almost any savory condiment or sauce you love. The trick is to keep the sauce between the skin and the flesh, because the layer of fat in the skin helps the chicken retain its moisture while the flavors in the marinade (green chutney, in this case) penetrate the flesh. The combination of spices and acid in the chutney helps tenderize the chicken and flavor it simultaneously. Basting the chicken with the drippings and broth ensures that the meat will be tender, juicy, and flavorful.

Crème Fraîche Chicken Salad

I like to give my chicken salad bursts of hot, sweet, and sour flavors to keep things interesting. Enjoy this salad by itself or between slices of thick sourdough bread brushed with Roasted Garlic (page 259) or the Hot Green Chutney (page 277) and good-quality European-style butter. I use sugarcane molasses, which we get from Michael's farm. Unsulphured molasses makes a good substitute. It will add a brighter sweetness than blackstrap molasses, which is too bitter.

MAKES 4 SERVINGS (4 CUPS [680 G] CHICKEN SALAD)

2 Tbsp extra-virgin olive oil

2 boneless, skinless chicken breasts (12 oz [340 g] total)

Salt and ground white pepper

¼ tsp anardana (whole pomegranate seeds)

½ tsp coriander seeds

1 cup [200 g] Kefir Crème Fraîche (page 260)

1 cup [240 g] plain Greek yogurt

1 Tbsp fresh lemon juice

1 Tbsp unsulphured molasses

¼ tsp cayenne pepper

½ cup [70 g] chopped cashews

2 Tbsp dried blueberries

1 Thai chile, seeded, if desired, and minced

2 Tbsp minced shallot

2 Tbsp julienned celeriac greens

2 Tbsp julienned carrot greens

8 slices sourdough bread, toasted, for serving

Frank's hot sauce, Tabasco, or your favorite hot sauce for serving (optional)

Heat the olive oil in a medium skillet over medium-high heat. Pat the chicken breasts dry with paper towels and season them on both sides with salt and pepper. Cook the chicken until evenly browned and the internal temperature reaches 165°F [74°C] on an instant-read thermometer, 5 to 6 minutes per side. Transfer the chicken to a plate or cutting board, cover, and cool completely. Cut the chicken into ½ in [12 mm] cubes and set aside. (You can cook the chicken up to 1 day ahead and store, covered, in the refrigerator.)

THE APPROACH Toasting the anardana and coriander seeds makes them smokier and nuttier, which helps the fat in the yogurt and crème fraîche carry their flavors even farther. The cashews, dried blueberries, and minced chiles add pops of flavor and texture. I prefer dried blueberries to raisins here because they're less sweet and provide a hint of tartness. Pomegranate molasses can be used instead of unsulphured molasses, if you want to add another fruity dimension to the salad.

Heat a small skillet over medium-high heat. Toast the anardana and coriander seeds until fragrant, swirling the spices occasionally so they toast evenly,
30 to 45 seconds. Remove from the heat, transfer to a mortar and pestle or
a spice grinder, and grind to a coarse powder. Transfer to a large bowl and
add the crème fraîche, yogurt, lemon juice, molasses, cayenne, and ¼ tsp
white pepper. Whisk to combine. Fold in the chicken, cashews, blueberries,
Thai chile, shallot, celeriac and carrot greens, and ½ tsp salt. Taste and
adjust the seasoning, if necessary. Serve with toasted bread and hot sauce, if
desired, on the side.

Turkey Leg Roast with Mixed Citrus and Juniper

When I was working on a story for my column in the *San Francisco Chronicle*, I did some research on juniper berries. I was fascinated to learn that Native Americans prized them for the piney, peppery notes they imparted to food. Ever since, I've been using juniper to season all sorts of soups and stews, and I've discovered that it also does wonders for poultry and game. Don't waste money on a fancy baster for this recipe: a large ladle works just as well, if not better.

MAKES 2 SERVINGS

2 large oranges

1 cup [240 ml] low-sodium chicken stock

Juice of 1 lemon

2 tsp dried juniper berries, ground

1 tsp cayenne pepper

1 tsp garlic powder

1 tsp fine sea salt

½ tsp freshly ground black pepper

3 oz [85 g] kumquats (about 12), halved crosswise and seeded

2 to 3 garlic bulbs, halved crosswise

Two 3½ lb [1.6 kg] turkey legs, with skin

Grate the zest of one orange and put it in a medium bowl. Squeeze and strain the juice from both oranges into the same bowl. Add the stock, lemon juice, juniper berries, cayenne, garlic powder, salt, and pepper. Transfer to a 9 by 13 in [23 by 33 cm] baking dish. Put the kumquats and garlic bulbs into the liquid and add the turkey legs. Cover the dish and refrigerate for 4 to 6 hours, occasionally spooning the marinade over the turkey.

Preheat the oven to 350°F [180°C]. Uncover the baking dish and transfer to the hot oven. Roast the turkey for 1½ to 2 hours, until the skin is golden brown and the internal temperature reaches 180°F [82°C] on an instant-read thermometer, basting the turkey occasionally with the liquid in the pan. Serve hot or warm.

THE APPROACH With its assertive flavor and aroma, a little juniper goes a long way. Here the juniper, garlic, and citrus all penetrate the meat, infusing it with flavor. As the turkey cooks, the liquids in the baking dish reduce into a concentrated broth. Basting the meat with it makes it extra moist and flavorful.

Turkey with Cherry-Fennel Barbecue Sauce

The best barbecue sauces are a carefully balanced blend of fruity, acidic, sweet, and hot notes. Here the combination of sour cherries and sweet Bings is perfect for grilled turkey, though you can pair it with any kind of meat. (It makes a mean pulled pork.)

MAKES 4 SERVINGS (2 CUPS [480 ML] BARBECUE SAUCE)

Cherry-Fennel Barbecue Sauce

½ lb [230 g] pitted fresh or frozen sour cherries

½ lb [230 g] pitted fresh or frozen sweet Bing cherries

½ cup [70 g] diced onion

¼ cup [60 g] spicy yellow mustard

2 Tbsp red wine vinegar

4 black peppercorns

½ tsp fennel seeds

1 tsp ground Kashmiri chile

½ cup [100 g] packed jaggery or muscovado sugar

½ tsp fine sea salt

4 lb [1.8 kg] bone-in turkey thighs, with skin

To make the barbecue sauce: In a blender or food processor, combine the cherries, onion, mustard, vinegar, peppercorns, fennel seeds, and chile powder and pulse on high speed until smooth. Transfer to a heavy medium saucepan and stir in the jaggery and salt. Cook over medium-high heat, stirring occasionally, until the jaggery is completely dissolved and the mixture starts to bubble. Remove from the heat. Taste and adjust seasoning if necessary. (The cooled sauce may be refrigerated for up to 1 month.)

Pat the turkey dry with paper towels. Using a small paring knife, prick it in a few places. Place in a large resealable plastic bag and add 1 cup [240 ml] of the barbecue sauce, reserving the rest for serving. Seal the bag, massage a few times, and refrigerate for at least 6 hours, and preferably overnight.

The next day, preheat the grill to high. Brush the grill grate lightly with oil and grill the turkey thighs directly on the hot grill for 15 to 20 minutes on each side, basting occasionally with the remaining 1 cup [240 ml] barbecue sauce. The turkey is cooked once the internal temperature registers 180°F [82°C] on an instant-read thermometer. Transfer to a serving platter and let sit for 5 to 10 minutes. Serve hot with the reserved barbecue sauce on the side.

THE APPROACH Jaggery is one of the few ingredients with imperfections and impurities that actually make it taste better. Its complex flavor is a combination of earthy, mineral, a little salty, and sweet. The vinegar and cherries provide acid while the fennel seeds add a hint of warmth and notes of licorice. The sugars in the sauce start to toast and caramelize as the turkey cooks, creating concentrated flavors that are deep and complex.

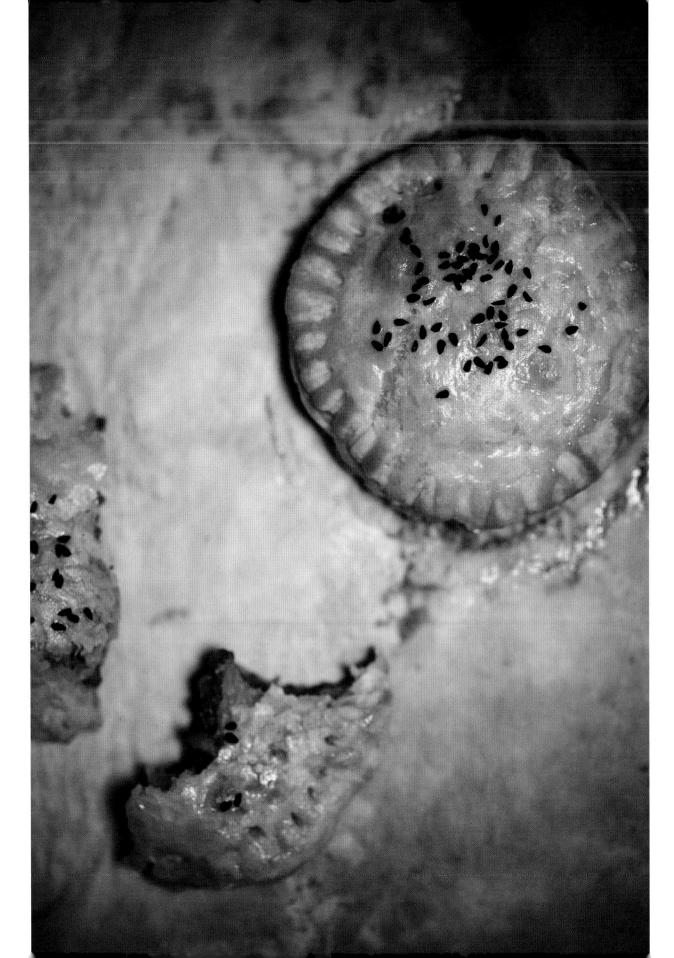

Turkey–Mushroom Hand Pies

These hand pies were my favorite snack in high school, and even though I've moved across oceans and continents, they continue to thrill me. During high school, I'd stop by the local Goan bakery every week to grab one or two of these delicious spiced ground meat "patties." When I couldn't find an equivalent here in America, I set about creating my own.

MAKES 8 INDIVIDUAL PIES

2 Tbsp extra-virgin olive oil

½ cup [70 g] finely diced white onion

½ tsp ground Kashmiri chile

½ tsp ground chipotle chile

1 garlic clove, minced

1 Thai chile, seeded, if desired, and thinly sliced

1 cup [90 g] sliced cremini mushrooms

1 lb [455 g] ground turkey

2 Tbsp coconut or apple cider vinegar

1 tsp fine sea salt

2 sheets frozen puff pastry, thawed

1 large egg

1 Tbsp water

2 Tbsp nigella seeds

Heat the oil in a large skillet over medium-high heat. Add the onion and sauté until translucent, 4 to 5 minutes. Add the Kashmiri chile, chipotle, and garlic and cook until fragrant, 30 to 45 seconds. Add the Thai chile and mushrooms and continue to sauté for 2 to 3 minutes more. Crumble in the ground turkey and cook, stirring occasionally, until the turkey is cooked through, 12 to 15 minutes. Stir in the vinegar and salt, raise the heat to high, and cook until most of the liquid has evaporated, about 5 minutes more. Taste and adjust the seasoning, if necessary. Cool to room temperature. (The filling may be prepared 1 day ahead. Cover and refrigerate.)

Continued

THE APPROACH I like to garnish these pies with nigella seeds, because they make a crunchy and flavorful complement to the rich dough. The vinegar brings the spices in the filling into sharp focus, and its acidity helps cure the meat as it cooks on the stove top. The chipotle adds a smoky touch.

To assemble the hand pies, line two baking sheets with parchment paper. Working with one sheet of pastry at a time (keep the other refrigerated), roll out the puff pastry on a clean and lightly floured surface. Using a 4 in [10 cm] round cookie or biscuit cutter, cut out sixteen pastry circles. Place 2 Tbsp of the cooled turkey-mushroom mixture in the center of each round. Brush the edges of the pastry with a little water and place a second piece of pastry on top, pressing the edges together gently to seal. Using the prongs of a fork, crimp the edges. Carefully transfer the filled pastries to the prepared baking sheet. Refrigerate while repeating with the second puff pastry sheet. Once all pies are formed, freeze for 10 to 12 minutes.

Preheat the oven to 350°F [180°C]. In a small bowl, whisk together the egg and 1 Tbsp water. Brush the top of each pie with egg wash and sprinkle a pinch of nigella seeds on top. Refrigerate for 10 minutes.

Bake the pies for 12 to 15 minutes, rotating the baking sheet halfway through baking, until they turn golden brown. Serve hot or warm.

My Approach

When I moved to America and began experimenting in the kitchen, I noticed that while there were obvious differences between the ingredients and techniques used in Indian and Western cooking, there were also strong similarities. When I made my curries, stews, and soups, I first cooked aromatics like onions, garlic, and ginger in hot fat, just as Westerners do, and then added spices. And like Westerners, I added fresh herbs at the end as a finishing touch, sometimes with a squeeze of fresh lemon or lime juice.

But I did notice that Indian cooks approach seasonings differently. They tend to rely on contrasting flavors, while Westerners paired similar tastes. I started to play with ingredients that were new to me, and transformed them with the techniques I learned in India. If I made a fresh tomato salad, I'd season it by toasting and grinding cumin and coriander seeds and drizzle the tomatoes with hot chile oil to produce a combination of hot, salty, smoky, and umami notes. Sometimes, I'd sprinkle red chili flakes and maple syrup over grilled bananas and serve them with vanilla ice cream. My two distinct worlds were coming together through aroma and taste.

Essential Techniques

Following are the techniques I use most often in my kitchen.

GRINDING

This is one of the simplest but most effective ways of transforming a spice or another ingredient into a seasoning agent. The crushing action breaks down the structure and releases the flavors. I use a sturdy mortar and pestle to grind most dry and wet ingredients. (A spice mill or coffee grinder is more effective for dried edible rose petals and cinnamon sticks.) To get a fine powder with a mortar and pestle, add a small quantity of an abrasive, such as salt or sugar. You can also crush many whole spices, including peppercorns and cardamom seeds, by putting them in a small resealable plastic bag, and pressing on them with something heavy, like a cast-iron skillet. Because grinding breaks down ingredients into tiny particles, it reduces their shelf life, so grind whole spices as needed to enjoy their full potency. When I need to grind spices and herbs in large batches for a condiment, such as Hot Green Chutney (page 277), I usually resort to a high-speed blender, which gets the job done in seconds.

BRUISING AND CHOPPING

I bruise herbs and spices before I use them to flavor oils. To bruise herbs, gently rub the stems and leaves between your palms, or bend and break them to release their flavor. For softer ingredients, such as garlic or cardamom, I often take the flat end of my knife and I rub the outer husk just enough to open it up and let the flavor do its magic.

TOASTING

One way to reduce the bitterness of a spice like cumin (pictured, top) or raise its flavor profile is to toast it before grinding. Toasting is also a good way to revive the flavors of dried spices that have been sitting in your pantry for a while. All you need is a dry skillet or saucepan. Heat the skillet over medium-high heat, add the spice, and toast until they just start to release their aroma and turn brown, swirling the spice occasionally so it toasts evenly. Do be vigilant, though. Spices burn quickly. The darker the spice, the faster it absorbs heat, which is why black peppercorns burn faster than coriander seeds. As soon as you start to smell the spice's aromatic compounds, remove the skillet from the heat and transfer the warm spice to a plate to cool. You can then grind the toasted spice or use it whole. Coriander (pictured, lower middle), fennel (pictured, bottom), and fenugreek (pictured, upper middle) also benefit greatly from toasting, and so does most fragrant rice (such as basmati and jasmine) and dried chiles (but these burn easily so watch them closely).

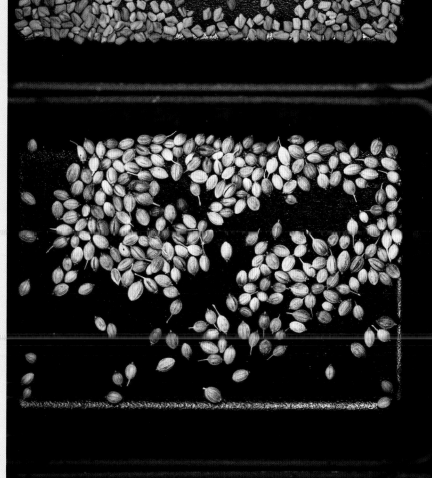

Tempering (called *tadka* in Hindi, and pictured, facing page) is another form of toasting, which is used in Indian cooking to mellow the flavor of a spice and to garnish a dish. (It should not to be confused with tempering eggs or chocolate with hot liquids.) A spice is added to an oil or a fat, such as coconut oil or Ghee (page 268), and the pan is placed over high heat. As the oil becomes hot, it absorbs the flavor of the spice. The flavored oil with its spice is then drizzled over the dish. See, for example, the Tandoori Swordfish Steaks (page 127).

INFUSING

Infusing is a way to extract flavor from an ingredient with the help of a solvent, such as water, alcohol, or oil. Varying the temperature and type of the solvent causes different flavor molecules to be extracted from the cells of the ingredient, which in turn affects the taste and aroma of the solvent. The most common example is vanilla extract, which is made commercially by steeping the tiny vanilla beans in hot alcohol. Adding hot water to tea leaves and spices for chai (page 264) is another way to infuse a liquid with flavor. To make rhubarb confit (page 278), oil is slowly infused with rhubarb, chiles, and garlic for hours in a low oven.

MUDDLING

When you muddle an ingredient, you are bruising, grinding, and infusing at the same time. A wooden or metal muddler, which is shaped like a pestle, is used to rub or crush an ingredient in a solvent to release its flavor molecules. Bartenders often muddle fresh herbs in alcohol to make cocktails. As the cells break under applied pressure, flavor molecules bind to the alcohol in the drink. The amount of pressure needed depends entirely on the herb. Some, like mint and basil, need only gentle pressure and will turn black if you overdo it. Thicker herbs like rosemary and sage require a little more pressure to release their full potential.

SMOKING

I sometimes smoke my food, especially when I'm grilling. Often when meats and vegetables are smoked, the smoke from burning wood deposits a layer of tarry molecules on the seasoned steak, protecting it from bacteria while adding a complex dimension of flavor. Uncooked meats are usually treated with a combination of smoke and heat, but some cooked foods, such as seafood, are cold smoked. The food is kept in a separate chamber so that it gets the smoke from the burning wood, but not the heat.

At home, I use dry sawdust instead of wood chips—a trick I picked up at the Culinary Institute of America at Greystone, in California—because sawdust burns faster. Some cooks prefer to soak the wood chips in water before adding them to the grill, so the wood won't burn as fast. I find this works best when food needs to be smoked for several hours.

BRINING, MARINATING, AND APPLYING RUBS

Indian and Western cooks use brines, marinades, and rubs to flavor meat, poultry, and seafood. The presence of salt and sugar (and sometimes acid) in the brines helps season these proteins through infusion, diffusion, and/or osmosis. To reduce the amount of time a food needs to sit in a brine or marinade, use a smaller and thinner cut, which will have more surface area and move the process along more quickly.

Brines are a combination of liquid and salt, to which sugar and spices or herbs are often added. A brine provides the meat with extra liquid, making it juicier, and it also adds flavor if the brine contains aromatics. The salt helps dissolve some of the meat's proteins, which allows the flavors in the brine to penetrate.

Marinades generally contain an acid, such as vinegar, yogurt, or citrus juice, and seasoning agents, such as salt, spices, and herbs. A marinade's acidity alters the proteins in the meat's tissues, allowing the flavor molecules to permeate the meat. It also tenderizes the meat, which speeds the cooking time. Some Indian and even Middle Eastern recipes will call for raw papaya in the marinade. Papaya contains an enzyme called papain, which helps

break down proteins and acts as a tenderizing agent. Be aware that meats sold pretenderized should marinate for less time, if at all, or they will take on an unpleasant texture. A long exposure to acid and enzymes breaks down the proteins in the meat's tissues too much.

Rubs are a combination of salt, sugar, and spices. They are applied dry, without any liquid, and flavor the meat on the surface. They can be used to cure food (see the gravlax on page 133) or on barbecued ribs and other cuts of meat that are smoked.

BROWNING

Browning is a technique we use frequently in the kitchen to add flavor and make food look more appealing, such as searing a steak in a hot skillet. One reason the seared steak tastes so good is the Maillard reaction, a reaction between the sugars in the meat and the amino acids, which make proteins. The Maillard reaction is responsible for that umami taste we all love—the blistered taste on naan and pizzas (pages 94 and 99), the unique nutty flavor of Ghee (page 268), and the browned bits of red meat at the bottom of a pan that make a beef stew so good (page 170).

Food containing sugar also browns at high temperatures through the process of caramelization: the sugar undergoes a physical and chemical transformation that results in a characteristically bittersweet caramel flavor. In the Rum-Soaked Raisin Caramel Cake (page 220), for example, the sugar is heated in a saucepan until it melts and becomes a deep shade of brown. In the recipe for grilled raisins and dates (page 33), the sugar inside the fruit actually burns and develops a bittersweet flavor and deep dark brown spots. Caramelization and the Maillard reaction can occur at the same time during cooking.

BRINGING IT ALL TOGETHER

When I create a recipe, I think about how I will flavor the ingredients at each stage. If I'm sautéing my onions and garlic first, I might temper my spices in the hot oil at the same time. Or I temper them at the end and pour the flavored oil over the dish. Sometimes I like to pair a hot component of a dish with a cool one, and season them separately. For example, in the broiled peaches dessert on page 200, the peaches are first caramelized under high heat. They are served warm with a dollop of cool crème fraîche flavored with vanilla beans and are drizzled with a sweet-and-sour maple-vinegar syrup at room temperature, which is infused with toasted spices.

At the end of most recipes in this book, I've added a brief note called The Approach, which explains why I chose a particular technique or seasoning. Armed with an understanding of this process, I encourage you to use the recipes included here as a guide, and experiment as much and as often as you can.

CHAPTER 6: Meat

While a good steak, or a rack of lamb, or pork chops can be seasoned simply with just a generous sprinkling of salt and freshly cracked pepper, there are many ways to make it more interesting. Rub the meat with cracked coriander seeds, garam masala, and a little dried orange peel (see page 173). Cook your meat with ghee or duck fat instead of olive oil. Or season it with a flaky smoked salt and serve it with Hot Green Chutney (page 277) or Sweet and Smoky Tahini Sauce (page 278).

Use cuts of meat with the bone left in; this is a wonderful and easy way to add an extra boost of flavor when making broths and stews. For special events, consider splurging on dry-aged beef or lamb. Dry-aging allows the meat to become more tender and tasty. The meat's exposure to air over a period of time dehydrates it and concentrates its flavor, while the natural enzymes in the tissue break down the protein and tenderize the meat.

Trying adding fresh or dried herbs when cooking ground meat; they will brighten the flavor. You can also play around with heat by using different kinds of chiles, from *urfa biber* flakes, with their chocolatelike aroma, to the smoky notes of chipotle. For more umami, consider using dried mushrooms or even tea or coffee to create a bolder taste.

I try to make the same conscious choices when I buy meat as I do when I buy poultry and eggs. I have a couple of trusted butchers whose stores I visit during the week, and on the weekends, I buy meat at the farmers' market.

Spiced Meat Loaf

Meat loaf is an iconic American dish with European origins, which has become one of my favorite meals to make at home because it's so adaptable. And it has personal significance for me because it's the first dish Michael cooked for me. My aromatic version offers a hint of heat, a bit of sourness, and an unexpected whisper of sweetness.

Because ground meat releases a lot of water when cooked, I prefer to bake the shaped loaf directly on a baking sheet, which helps the liquid evaporate during cooking. If you can get your hands on a special meat loaf pan with a perforated insert, you can use that instead.

MAKES 8 SERVINGS

Meat Loaf

2 Tbsp unsalted butter

2 cups [280 g] finely diced onion

4 garlic cloves, grated

One 1 in [2.5 cm] piece fresh ginger, peeled and grated

1½ tsp garam masala, homemade (page 263) or store-bought

1 tsp ground coriander

1 tsp cayenne pepper

2 Granny Smith apples, peeled and grated

1 cup [40 g] packed chopped fresh mint

1 cup [40 g] packed chopped fresh flat-leaf parsley

½ cup [70 g] dry bread crumbs

1½ tsp fine sea salt

1 tsp freshly ground black pepper

2 lb [910 g] ground beef (15 percent fat)

1½ Tbsp Worcestershire sauce

2 large eggs, lightly beaten

Glaze

¼ cup [65 g] ketchup

1 Tbsp pomegranate molasses

1 Tbsp jaggery or muscovado sugar

1 tsp amchur

½ tsp cayenne pepper

½ tsp fine sea salt

Continued

THE APPROACH This meat loaf has layers of flavor. The garam masala and cayenne add heat to the beef, the Granny Smith apples add sweet-tart notes, and the Worcestershire sauce bumps up the umami. The pomegranate molasses gives the glaze a sour contour, while the jaggery and amchur (ground dried unripe mango) lend it a fruity flavor, which goes beautifully with the spiced beef.

To assemble the meat loaf: In a large saucepan, melt the butter over medium-high heat. Sauté the onion until translucent, 4 to 5 minutes. Add the garlic, ginger, garam masala, coriander, and cayenne and cook, stirring constantly, until fragrant, 30 to 45 seconds. Remove from the heat, transfer to a large bowl, and cool for 10 minutes. Squeeze the grated apples and discard the juice. Add the apples, mint, parsley, bread crumbs, salt, and black pepper to the bowl with the onion mixture, stirring gently with a large wooden spoon or rubber spatula. Add the ground beef, Worcestershire sauce, and eggs, and stir to combine. Shape the loaf by hand and place it on an aluminum foil–lined baking sheet or in a 9 in [23 cm] loaf pan with a perforated insert. Cover and refrigerate for 30 minutes.

To make the glaze: Combine all the ingredients in a small saucepan. Bring to a boil over high heat, stirring constantly, and then remove from heat.

Preheat the oven to 400°F [200°C]. Bake the meat loaf in the oven for 1 hour. Spread the glaze over the surface of the loaf, and return it to the oven for another 25 to 30 minutes, or until it registers 160°F [71°C] on an instant-read thermometer and is slightly firm to the touch. Let sit for at least 10 minutes and serve hot or warm.

Beef Stew with Verjus

While a bowl of warm beef stew with falling-apart tender meat is comforting, there's no reason it can't have an exciting taste. Here the beef bathes in an aromatic bath flavored with cinnamon, garlic, and the fruity acidity of verjus, pomegranate molasses, and dry red wine. This is my ode to California wine country.

MAKES 4 SERVINGS

1¼ lb [570 g] pearl onions

¼ cup [60 ml] extra-virgin olive oil

2 lb [910 g] beef chuck, cut into 1 in [2.5 cm] cubes

2 Tbsp minced garlic

2 bay leaves, fresh or dried

One 2 in [5 cm] cinnamon stick

1 Tbsp tomato paste

2 Tbsp verjus rouge (red verjus)

2 Tbsp pomegranate molasses

1 cup [240 ml] dry red wine, such as Pinot Noir

1 tsp fine sea salt

½ tsp freshly ground black pepper

Cooked rice (page 256) or Naan (page 94) for serving (optional)

Fill a medium saucepan with water and bring to a rolling boil. Fill a medium bowl with ice water. Using a paring knife, trim both ends of the pearl onions and plunge the onions into the boiling water for 30 seconds. Using a slotted spoon, transfer to the ice water to stop the cooking. Drain and put the onions on a clean kitchen towel or paper towels and dab them dry. Pinch the stem ends of the onions and slip off the skins.

In a large, heavy Dutch oven over medium-high heat, heat the olive oil. Add the onions and sauté until they start to turn golden, 5 to 6 minutes. Using a slotted spoon, remove the onions and drain on paper towels.

THE APPROACH When the beef and onions are cooked in very hot oil, the chemical Maillard reaction occurs, resulting in flavor compounds that add depth and aroma to the stew. The oil also helps release the aromatic flavors of the bay leaves, cinnamon, and garlic. Then, as the stew simmers, the combined acidity of the pomegranate molasses, verjus, and red wine tenderize the beef by breaking down its collagen.

Pat the meat dry with paper towels. Increase the heat to high and add the meat cubes to the Dutch oven. Brown the beef deeply on all sides, 4 to 5 minutes. Stir in the garlic, bay leaves, and cinnamon stick and cook until fragrant, 30 to 45 seconds. Stir in the tomato paste and cook for 30 seconds more. Add the verjus, pomegranate molasses, and red wine and bring to a rolling boil, scraping up the browned bits from the bottom of the pot. Turn the heat to medium-low, add the salt and pepper, and cover the pot. Simmer until the beef is tender, stirring occasionally, about 1 hour. Taste and adjust the seasoning, if necessary. Stir in the browned pearl onions and cook for 10 minutes longer. Serve hot or warm, with rice or naan, if desired. (You can remove the whole spices before serving, but I usually prefer to leave them in.)

Steak with Orange Peel and Coriander

I call this spice combo my house seasoning because I turn to it every time I cook steak. Guests can never put their finger on exactly what's going on, which gives the dish added intrigue.

MAKES 4 SERVINGS

2 Tbsp dried orange peel

2 Tbsp garam masala, homemade (page 263) or store-bought

1 Tbsp coriander seeds

2½ tsp kosher salt

Two 1 in [2.5 cm] thick T-bone steaks (1½ to 2 lb [680 to 910 g] each)

2 to 4 Tbsp Ghee (page 268), melted

Crush the orange peel, garam masala, and coriander with a mortar and pestle. Stir in the salt.

Pat the steaks dry with paper towels, and rub the spice generously on both sides of the steaks. Cover with plastic wrap and refrigerate for at least 6 hours, and preferably overnight.

When you're ready to cook, preheat the grill to high and brush the grates with a little oil. Drizzle about 1 Tbsp of ghee on each side of the steaks. Slap them on the hot grill, close the lid, and cook the steaks until done the way you like them, 3 to 4 minutes per side for rare and 5 to 6 minutes per side for medium-rare (120°F [49°C] for rare and 130°F [54°C] for medium-rare on an instant-read thermometer). Or, if using a grill pan, heat 2 Tbsp of the ghee over high heat until smoking and cook the steaks, one at a time. Transfer the steaks to a plate, tent loosely with foil, and let sit for 5 minutes before serving.

THE APPROACH I tend to find red meat a little heavy, so I choose seasonings that lighten its flavor. Dried orange peel and garam masala both add brightness. Kosher salt does a wonderful job of drawing the liquid out from the steak, which will help create an exceptional crust.

Ground Lamb and Potato "Chops" with Sambal Oelek

I think of potato chops as little parcels of joy. There is no better way to combine meat and potatoes than this Goan specialty. Imagine your fork piercing a pan-fried coating of crisp bread crumbs and sinking into a layer of smooth mashed potatoes and then juicy, spiced ground meat. If you have any left over, enjoy them for breakfast. Top each one with a fried egg and a big spoonful of Hot Green Chutney (page 277). You can find sambal oelek, a chile-based Indonesian condiment, in many grocery stores and most Asian markets.

MAKES 6 SERVINGS

2 Tbsp extra-virgin olive oil

1 cup [140 g] minced red onion

1 Tbsp minced garlic

One 1 in [2.5 cm] piece fresh ginger, peeled and grated

1 lb [455 g] ground lamb

1½ tsp fine sea salt

2 Tbsp apple cider vinegar

1½ Tbsp sambal oelek

2 Tbsp chopped fresh cilantro

2 lb [910 g] russet potatoes

½ tsp freshly ground black pepper

1 large egg

2 cups [280 g] dry bread crumbs

¼ cup [60 ml] vegetable oil

Heat the olive oil in a large skillet with a cover over medium-high heat. Add the onion and sauté until translucent, 4 to 5 minutes. Stir in the garlic and ginger and cook until fragrant, 30 to 45 seconds. Break up the ground lamb into small chunks and add it to the skillet. Brown the meat for 5 to 6 minutes. Add ½ tsp of the salt, the vinegar, and the sambal oelek and stir gently to combine. Cover and cook, stirring occasionally, until most of the liquid has evaporated, 10 to 12 minutes, Remove from the heat and cool to room temperature. Stir in the cilantro and adjust the seasoning, if necessary. (The lamb filling may be prepared 1 day ahead. Cover and refrigerate.)

Continued

THE APPROACH If you don't care for lamb, or red meat in general, you can substitute ground chicken or turkey. In the traditional Goan version of this dish, the meat is flavored with a combination of spices and coconut vinegar. I like to include sambal oelek and apple cider vinegar, which makes all the flavors pop.

While the lamb is cooking, scrub the potatoes and put them in a large stock-pot. Add enough cool water to cover by 1 in [2.5 cm]. Bring to a rolling boil, turn the heat to medium-low, and cover. Simmer the potatoes until completely tender, 20 to 25 minutes. Carefully drain off the water and allow the potatoes to cool to room temperature. (The potatoes may be prepared 1 day ahead. Cover and refrigerate.)

Peel the potatoes and, with a masher or fork (or a ricer if you prefer a smoother texture), mash until there are no visible chunks left behind. Season with the remaining 1 tsp salt and the pepper. Taste and adjust the seasoning, if necessary.

To assemble the chops, take 3 or 4 generous Tbsp of the mashed potatoes in the palms of your hands and flatten into a disk. Put 1½ to 2 Tbsp of the lamb filling in the center, and fold the edges of the potato around it to form a patty 1½ to 2 in [4 to 5 cm] in diameter. Place on a sheet of parchment paper and repeat with the remaining meat and potatoes.

Whisk the egg in a small bowl. Spread out the bread crumbs on a baking sheet. Using a pastry brush, brush a patty with the egg and coat evenly with the bread crumbs, shaking off the excess. Repeat with the remaining patties.

Heat 1 to 2 Tbsp of the vegetable oil in a nonstick or cast-iron skillet over medium-low heat. Cook the patties in batches, adding more oil as needed, until golden brown, 4 to 5 minutes per side. Drain on a paper towels. Serve hot or warm.

Lamb Chops with Red Lentils

Two of the most popular sources of protein in Indian cuisine are goat or mutton and lentils. So it's no surprise that they appear together in dishes enjoyed across India, from the Parsi *dhansak* to the *dal gosht* cooked in many north Indian homes. Inspired by tradition, I created this dish, which features lamb (a good substitute for goat) chops served over a spiced red lentil stew. A bowl of plain rice is the ideal accompaniment.

MAKES 4 SERVINGS

Lentils

½ cup [100 g] red lentils, picked over for stones

2 Tbsp vegetable oil

½ cup [70 g] finely diced white onion

2 garlic cloves, minced

1 Tbsp grated peeled fresh ginger

2 dried whole Kashmiri chiles

½ tsp ground cumin

½ tsp freshly ground black pepper

½ tsp ground turmeric

1 tsp dried thyme

1 tsp dried oregano

1 large tomato, diced

1 tsp fine sea salt

2 cups [480 ml] water

Lamb Chops

4 lamb loin chops (about 1½ lb [680 g] total)

1 tsp ground Kashmiri chile

1 tsp fine sea salt

1 tsp freshly ground black pepper

4 Tbsp extra-virgin olive oil

Continued

THE APPROACH I've done what I call a "reverse-*tadka*" in this recipe. Traditional dals and other stews in Indian cuisine are drizzled with a seasoned hot oil or *tadka* (see page 161) after they're cooked. Here, though, the spices, dried herbs, and lentils are cooked together.

To make the lentils: Rinse the lentils in a fine mesh strainer under cold running water. Heat the oil in a medium saucepan over medium-high heat. Add the onion and sauté for 4 to 5 minutes, until translucent. Add the garlic and ginger and cook, stirring, until fragrant, 30 to 45 seconds. Stir in the chiles, cumin, black pepper, turmeric, thyme, and oregano and cook for 30 seconds more. Add the tomato and cook for 2 minutes, stirring occasionally. Add the lentils, salt, and water. Increase the heat to high and bring to a rolling boil. Lower the heat and cook, covered, until the lentils are tender, 35 to 40 minutes. Taste and adjust the seasoning, if necessary. Transfer the lentils to a serving bowl, tent with aluminum foil, and keep warm.

To make the lamb chops: Pat the chops dry with paper towels. In a small bowl, stir together the ground chile, salt, pepper, and 2 Tbsp of the olive oil and massage over the chops. Cover and refrigerate for 30 minutes. Heat the remaining 2 Tbsp olive oil in a nonstick or cast-iron skillet over medium-high heat. Place the lamb chops in the hot skillet and cook until they're well browned on each side and their internal temperature registers 145°F [63°C] on an instant-read thermometer for medium-rare, 160°F [71°C] for medium, or 170°F [77°C] for well done. Remove the chops from the skillet and serve warm atop the lentil stew. (You can remove the chiles before serving, but I usually prefer to leave them in.)

Roast Leg of Lamb

People are always surprised when I tell them that many Indians eat red meat, especially goat. *Raan* is perhaps the most glamorous testament to this affection. The word *raan* refers to a goat's hind legs, which are tenderized by the acids in a buttermilk- or yogurt-based marinade and then slow-cooked until the meat is falling off the bone. My take on this classic dish is made with lamb instead of goat—it's so much easier to find and work with—and a mixture of nuts and white wine. Because this lamb roast is rich, I serve it with cooked rice (page 256) or Naan (page 94), cucumber salad (page 59), and some plain yogurt on the side.

MAKES 4 SERVINGS

5 lb [2.3 kg] bone-in leg of lamb

1 cup [240 g] plain full-fat yogurt, plus more for serving

Juice of 1 lemon

½ cup [70 g] almonds

½ cup [70 g] shelled pistachios

One 3 in [7.5 cm] piece fresh ginger, peeled

10 garlic cloves, peeled

8 whole cloves

Seeds from 10 green cardamom pods, crushed

5 juniper berries

1 tsp black peppercorns

2 tsp ground turmeric

2 Tbsp honey

2¼ tsp kosher salt

1 cup [240 ml] white wine

2 Tbsp Ghee (page 268), melted

2 Tbsp fresh mint leaves

Pat the lamb dry with paper towels. Trim and discard any excess fat. Using a sharp knife, score the meat by making shallow cuts. Put the lamb in a large resealable plastic bag and set aside.

Continued

THE APPROACH Due to their high oil content, the nuts enrich the spiced yogurt soak, and they add flavor. Because the lamb is marinated for a long time and then braised, the meat is falling-apart tender and exceptionally juicy.

In a blender, combine the yogurt, lemon juice, nuts, ginger, garlic, cloves, cardamom, juniper, peppercorns, turmeric, honey, and salt. Pulse on high speed until smooth. Pour the marinade into the bag, press out the air, and seal. Massage the lamb to coat evenly with the marinade and refrigerate for at least 12 hours, and preferably 24 hours.

When you're ready to roast the lamb, preheat the oven to 350°F [180°C]. Grease a large roasting pan with a little vegetable oil. Put the lamb in the roasting pan and add the wine. Tent the pan with aluminum foil and roast the lamb for 1 hour. Remove the foil and return the pan to the oven for 30 minutes more, basting the lamb every 10 minutes with the pan juices. Increase the heat to 425°F [220°C] and roast the lamb until the meat starts to brown and the internal temperature registers 145°F [63°C] for medium-rare, 160°F [71°C] for medium, or 170°F [77°C] for well done on an instant-read thermometer, another 8 to 10 minutes. Remove the lamb from the oven and let it rest, covered with aluminum foil, for 10 minutes. Transfer the hot lamb to a platter, drizzle with the melted ghee, and garnish with the mint leaves.

Chaat Masala–Grilled Pork Chops

This dish is ridiculously simple to put together. Although chaat masala is used mostly to season vegetarian street food in Bombay, it works just as well for grilling pork. The smoky flavors of chaat masala and the meat play well against the acidic, hot, and sweet notes of the other ingredients featured here.

MAKES 2 SERVINGS

Capers and Piquillo Peppers

1 cup [140 g] roasted piquillo peppers, drained

⅓ cup [60 g] capers, drained

3 Tbsp minced shallot

2 Tbsp fresh flat-leaf parsley leaves

1 serrano chile, seeded, if desired, and minced

2 Tbsp verjus blanc (white verjus)

1 Tbsp extra-virgin olive oil

½ tsp freshly ground black pepper

Fine sea salt (optional)

Pork Chops

Two 1½ in [4 cm] thick bone-in, center-cut pork chops
    (about 1¾ lb [1.2 kg] total)

2 Tbsp fine sea salt

2 cups [480 ml] cold water

1 Tbsp Chaat Masala (page 263)

½ tsp freshly ground black pepper

2 Tbsp extra-virgin olive oil

To make the capers and piquillo peppers: In a medium bowl, toss all the ingredients together, except the salt. Taste and season with salt, if needed. Refrigerate for at least 30 minutes before serving.

To make the pork chops: Put the pork chops into a large resealable plastic bag. Stir the salt into the water, pour into the bag, and seal. Refrigerate for 1 hour to brine. Discard the brining solution and pat the pork chops dry with paper towels. In a small bowl, mix the chaat masala, and black pepper together and massage over the pork. Return to the refrigerator for 30 minutes.

THE APPROACH As the chaat masala hits the hot grill, it releases smoky notes into the meat. The fruity caper and piquillo pepper relish is a perfect foil for the pork chops, delivering acid, salt, and heat.

Meanwhile, preheat the grill to high and brush the grates with oil. Drizzle the 2 Tbsp olive oil on both sides of the pork chops, and cook until their internal temperature reaches 135°F [57°C] on an instant-read thermometer, 3 to 5 minutes per side. Or, if using a grill pan, heat the pan over medium-high heat, add the olive oil, and cook the chops. Serve with the capers and piquillo peppers on the side.

Pulled Pork Tacos with Apple and Serrano Slaw

A few years ago, when Michael and I drove cross-country on our big move from Washington, D.C., to San Francisco, we ate some of the best tacos we've ever had. Made by street vendors in Southern California, these tacos were packed with flavor. They are the inspiration behind these pulled pork tacos, a perfect combination of hot and sour blended with the earthy sweetness of jaggery.

MAKES 4 SERVINGS (2 CUPS [210 G] SLAW)

Pulled Pork

3 lb [1.4 kg] boneless pork butt

1 medium onion, peeled and quartered

2 cups [480 ml] white wine

¼ cup [50 g] jaggery

¼ cup [60 ml] apple cider vinegar

2 Tbsp amchur

1½ tsp Kashmiri chile powder

6 black peppercorns

5 whole cloves

2 bay leaves

Seeds from 10 green cardamom pods, crushed

1 star anise pod

One 2 in [5 cm] piece fresh ginger, peeled

Apple and Serrano Slaw

2 large Granny Smith apples

¼ cup [60 ml] apple cider vinegar

1 Tbsp fresh lemon juice

2 Tbsp fresh cilantro leaves

2 Tbsp fresh mint leaves

1 serrano chile, seeded, if desired, and thinly sliced

½ tsp ground white pepper

½ tsp fine sea salt

8 to 12 corn or flour tortillas

1 or 2 limes, quartered, for serving

THE APPROACH Pork pairs well with sweet and sour flavors, especially those with fruitier profiles. Here amchur (ground dried unripe mango), apple cider vinegar, and white wine add tart notes, while the jaggery adds an earthy sweetness. By slow-cooking the pork butt with the spices in the acidic wine and vinegar, the meat becomes tender while absorbing the flavors of the liquid. The minty apple and serrano slaw brightens the tacos.

To make the pulled pork: Preheat the oven to 400°F [200°C]. Trim and discard any excess fat from the pork. Put the meat in a medium Dutch oven. Combine the remaining ingredients in a blender and blend at high speed until smooth. Pour over the pork. Wrap the lid of the Dutch oven with two to three sheets of aluminum foil, pressing and folding the edges tightly so that when you cover the pot, you create a seal. Put the lid on the Dutch oven. Cook the pork in the oven until tender and falling apart, 2½ to 3 hours. Remove from the oven and let cool for 1 to 2 hours. Refrigerate the pork in the Dutch oven overnight.

To make the slaw: Core, peel, and grate the apples, squeeze to remove any excess liquid, and transfer the grated apples to a medium bowl. Add the remaining ingredients, stir well, and taste to adjust the seasoning, if necessary. Cover with plastic wrap and refrigerate for 30 minutes before serving.

When ready to assemble the tacos, remove and discard any fat that has solidified on the surface of the pork and its liquid. Reheat on the stove top over medium-high heat. Warm the tortillas on a hot pan or by holding directly over a gas flame. To serve, place 1 to 2 generous Tbsp of pulled pork on each warm tortilla and add 1 tsp of the slaw. Serve with the limes for diners to squeeze on the taco as desired.

Homemade Goan-Style Chouriço

The Goan community in India takes great pride in Goa sausage, or Goan *chouriço* as it is sometimes called. Fatty bits of pork are cooked with spices and *feni*, a local country liquor, sort of like moonshine, obtained by the natural fermentation of the coconut tree's sap or the cashew fruit. The mixture is stuffed into casings and left to cure for several days. This spicy sausage is sautéed with vegetables, stuffed into naans (Michael's favorite way), and even used to flavor rice. Because it's difficult to source Goa sausage or *feni* here, I developed a simpler recipe, which I make with coconut vinegar. If you can't find it, use apple cider vinegar instead.

MAKES 1 LB [455 G]

1 tsp black peppercorns

½ tsp cumin seeds

3 whole cloves

1 lb [455 g] ground pork (preferably with fat)

¼ cup [60 ml] coconut vinegar

2 garlic cloves, minced

One 1 in [2.5 cm] piece fresh ginger, peeled and grated

1 Tbsp dried oregano

1 Tbsp ground Kashmiri chile

1 tsp cayenne pepper

1 tsp jaggery or brown sugar

1 tsp fine sea salt

¼ tsp ground cinnamon

Grind the black peppercorns, cumin seeds, and cloves with a mortar and pestle or a spice grinder and transfer to a large bowl. Add the remaining ingredients and mix with a fork to blend well. Shape into a log, wrap with wax paper or parchment paper, and refrigerate for at least 1 hour, and preferably overnight.

Cut off pieces of the *chouriço* as needed. Cook in a skillet over medium-high heat until the internal temperature reaches 160°F [73°C] on an instant-read thermometer, about 10 minutes. Tightly wrap the leftover *chouriço* in plastic wrap, slip into a resealable plastic bag, and store in the freezer for up to 1 month.

THE APPROACH Coconut vinegar is the key ingredient in this recipe, because it enhances the spiciness of the meat and also cures it. Ground Kashmiri chile gives the sausage its deep red color, while the cayenne bumps up the heat. When making sausages such as this *chouriço*, I don't toast the spices before grinding them because the vinegar's acidity releases their flavors quite effectively.

CHAPTER 7: Sweets

If I didn't love desserts, I would never have quit my day job to work in a patisserie. But my sweet tooth had been established at an early age. Our daily tea ritual at four in the afternoon always included some sort of snack or dessert, usually in the form of a pudding or a cake.

Indians have a fondness for sweets. My dad's family favors more traditional Indian desserts, many of which are dairy-based, while my mom's family makes a lot of Goan, Portuguese, and Western sweets, which tend to include eggs. Every Christmas and Easter, my mom and the women in her family would spend days making large marzipan treats, cookies, and cakes to share with our neighbors, friends, and family.

I like unfussy desserts with bold flavors and textures. When faced with a choice, I often pick sweets made with seasonal fruits. Part of the pleasure involves delayed gratification—waiting all year for fresh ripe peaches or melons to come into season, and then following my inspiration.

Spices, when used well, make desserts extra special. Many of the spices that we use in savory dishes will also work in sweet ones. I always joke that green cardamom, for example, is the Indian vanilla, because we use it to flavor almost every conceivable dessert. And black pepper adds depth to a rich and chocolaty hazelnut cookie (page 203). Spices can also be infused into hot liquids like milk when making ice cream (page 199).

Fruits are rich in sugar, which caramelizes under the broiler or in the oven, adding complexity to a dessert or cake. See, for example, the broiled peaches on page 200 and the rum-soaked raisin cake on page 220. Aromatic fats like ghee can be paired with aromatic blossoms like elderflowers or lavender for a cake (page 215). Fresh herbs can brighten up the flavor of many desserts and make for a refreshing finale, like the shiso used in my raspberry sorbet (page 196).

Whole grains add their own unique flavor and subtle sweetness, so I often use whole-wheat pastry flour in cakes and desserts. Even though it's rich in fiber, this flour has a lower gluten content than regular whole wheat flour, because it comes from white wheat. As a result, cakes made with it have a delicate crumb.

Finally, even sugars come in various flavors. I use jaggery a lot throughout this book (see page 253) because of its rich, earthy taste. And the fine layer of coconut palm sugar on the ghee cake (page 215) makes for a surprising and delicious finish.

Watermelon–Elderflower Granita

Watermelons are a delightful fruit, which I think Mother Nature created to help us get through the hot months of summer. The bold color and flaky texture of this watermelon granita get a flavorful lift from condensed coconut milk and the floral scent of elderflowers. Condensed coconut milk can be found at most grocery stores and Asian markets.

MAKES 6 TO 8 SERVINGS

One 2 lb [910 g] piece of seedless watermelon

¼ cup [50 g] sugar

¼ cup [60 ml] fresh lime juice

2 Tbsp elderflower liqueur

½ cup [120 ml] condensed coconut milk

Cut the watermelon into large chunks and put in a blender. Add the sugar, lime juice, and elderflower liqueur. Pulse until smooth and well combined. Pass through a fine-mesh strainer set over a bowl. Discard the solids in the strainer and pour the liquid into a metal baking pan or roasting pan. Cover with aluminum foil and freeze for 1 hour. Remove the pan from the freezer and stir the contents with a fork to break up the ice crystals that form as the liquid begins to freeze. Cover and return the pan to the freezer for 1 hour more. Remove the pan from the freezer and rake the ice crystals with the fork again, and return it to the freezer for another hour. Repeat this process two more times. (The granita is in the freezer for a total of 5 hours.) Rake the granita once more to get flaky crystals, cover with plastic wrap, and freeze until ready to serve. To serve, scrape the granita into glasses or bowls and drizzle each one with a generous Tbsp of the condensed coconut milk. Store the leftover granita in an airtight container in the freezer for up to 1 week. Flake the crystals with a fork just before serving.

THE APPROACH By itself, watermelon can taste a bit flat, so the fresh lime juice helps brighten and give added depth to the fruit. The elderflower liqueur adds a floral back note while the condensed coconut milk offers visual and textural contrast as well as a tropical flavor.

Raspberry-Shiso Sorbet

A few years ago, when we lived in Washington, D.C., my mom visited us for the first time, and we took her to pick raspberries at a U pick farm in the country. Competitiveness with our fellow pickers and plain old greed got the best of us, and we ended the day with a far larger haul than we could possibly eat. The solution? We froze all the leftover berries and later made raspberry sorbet.

MAKES 1 PT [480 ML]

1 cup [200 g] sugar

1 cup [240 ml] water

20 green shiso leaves

4 cups [480 g] fresh raspberries

1½ Tbsp fresh lemon juice

Line a fine-mesh strainer with cheesecloth and set aside.

In a small saucepan, bring the sugar and water to a rolling boil, stirring until the sugar dissolves. Remove the simple syrup from the heat. Add the shiso leaves and, with a muddler or wooden spoon, crush them into the syrup. Cover and steep for 2 hours at room temperature. Discard the leaves. Transfer the syrup to a blender, add the raspberries and lemon juice, and pulse until well combined. Set the cheesecloth-lined strainer over a bowl, and pass the sorbet base through the strainer, discarding the seeds left behind. Refrigerate or pour into a resealable plastic bag, and plunge into a bowl filled with ice water, until the sorbet base reaches 40°F [5°C] on an instant-read thermometer.

Transfer the sorbet base to an ice cream maker, and churn according to the manufacturer's instructions. Spoon into an airtight freezer-safe container and freeze until firm, at least 6 hours. To serve, leave the sorbet at room temperature for about 5 minutes before scooping. Store the leftover sorbet in the freezer for up to 1 week.

THE APPROACH Shiso is a member of the mint family and is commonly used in Japanese cooking. It comes in green and red varieties, both of which taste a little like spearmint. The green variety also has a hint of cinnamon, while the red has a whisper of anise. Muddling the leaves and then steeping them in the hot simple syrup ensures their flavor will permeate the sorbet.

Jaggery Ice Cream

Jaggery is a classic sweetener used in Indian cooking, and is made by evaporating sugarcane or date palm juice. The result is crumbly sugar with hints of molasses and a slightly salty finish. It comes in various shades of brown, and for this ice cream I prefer the lighter golden brown variety, which won't mask the golden tones of the saffron.

MAKES 6 TO 8 SERVINGS

Seeds from 2 green cardamom pods, crushed

½ cup [120 ml] whole milk

2½ cups [600 ml] heavy cream

⅔ cup [130 g] packed jaggery

¼ tsp saffron strands

6 egg yolks

Grind the cardamom seeds with a mortar and pestle or spice grinder. Transfer to a medium saucepan and add the milk, heavy cream, jaggery, and saffron strands. Heat over low heat until the jaggery is completely dissolved, 4 to 5 minutes. Remove from the heat.

In a small bowl, whisk the yolks. Add the yolks to the saucepan and whisk quickly until combined. Cook over low heat, stirring constantly, until the mixture thickens to a custardlike consistency and coats the back of a wooden spoon. (Your finger should leave a clean trail on the back of the spoon when you draw a line through the custard coating.) Continue to cook, stirring constantly, until the mixture reaches 185°F [85°C] on an instant-read thermometer. Remove from the heat. Set a fine-mesh strainer over a medium bowl and strain the ice cream base to remove any lumps. Transfer the saffron strands back into the custard. Transfer to a large resealable plastic bag and seal. Plunge the bag into a large bowl filled with ice water, and let it sit until the custard is completely chilled, about 30 minutes.

Transfer the ice cream base to an ice cream maker and churn according to the manufacturer's instructions. Scrape the ice cream into an airtight freezer-safe container, place a sheet of parchment paper cut to size against the surface of the ice cream, and freeze until firm, at least 2 to 4 hours. Leave the ice cream out for about 5 minutes to soften a little before serving. Store the leftover ice cream in the freezer for up to 5 days.

THE APPROACH Jaggery is an unrefined sweetener. It has an earthy taste, with hints of molasses, because it is rich in minerals. The green cardamom and saffron flavor the custard, and the saffron turns it a beautiful golden color. Green cardamom is a cooling spice, whose flavor becomes more potent in frozen desserts. Avoid the urge to use too many saffron threads, as they can quickly become overpowering.

Spiced Maple–Broiled Peaches

After I moved to America, juicy Southern peaches replaced that special spot I reserved in my heart for Indian mangoes. I prefer yellow peaches to white because they are a little tangier, and pair better with spices. The spiced sweet-and-sour maple syrup used to top these broiled peaches is also great with Curry Leaf Popcorn Chicken (page 48).

MAKES 6 SERVINGS

Spiced Maple-Vinegar Syrup

1 cup [240 ml] maple syrup

¼ cup [60 ml] apple cider vinegar

1 tsp rainbow peppercorns

1 tsp fennel seeds

1 tsp coriander seeds

Vanilla Bean Crème Fraîche

1 vanilla bean

1 cup [200 g] Kefir Crème Fraîche (page 260)

¼ cup [30 g] confectioners' sugar

Peaches

6 firm, ripe yellow peaches, halved and pitted

¼ cup [55 g] unsalted butter, melted

To make the syrup: In a small bowl, mix together the maple syrup and vinegar. Set aside. Heat a small skillet over high heat and add the peppercorns, fennel seeds, and coriander seeds. Toast until fragrant, swirling the spices occasionally so they toast evenly, 30 to 45 seconds. Remove from the heat and transfer the seeds to a mortar and pestle. Gently crack the seeds until coarse, and stir into the maple-vinegar syrup. Cover with plastic wrap and refrigerate for at least 2 hours, and preferably overnight.

To make the crème fraîche: Halve the vanilla bean lengthwise and scrape the seeds into a small bowl. Add the crème fraîche and confectioners' sugar, and whisk to combine. Cover with plastic wrap and refrigerate until ready to use.

To broil the peaches: Position a rack in the upper third of the oven and preheat the broiler. Brush the flesh of the peach halves with the melted butter and

THE APPROACH This recipe, inspired by the flavors of the American South and of India, offers interesting contrasts between flavors and temperatures. Peaches broiled with a light coating of butter become hot and crisp, while the scoop of crème fraîche is silky and cool. The sweet-and-sour syrup offers tang, underpinned with a warm infusion of mixed spices.

place them in a baking dish or on a baking sheet, skin-side down. Broil the peaches, watching carefully so they don't burn, until the tops start to caramelize and the juices bubble, 5 to 6 minutes. Transfer to a serving dish.

To serve, top each peach half with some of the chilled crème fraîche and a generous drizzle of the spiced maple-vinegar syrup. Serve immediately.

Spicy Chocolate Chip–Hazelnut Cookies

In the early eighteenth century, a marriage took place in Turin, Italy, and the world has never been quite the same ever since. I'm talking about the sacred union of chocolate and hazelnuts, ground together into what is called *gianduja*. It was born out of economic necessity, when cocoa was expensive, and hazelnuts became a filler. Be forewarned: these cookies are maddeningly good.

MAKES 1 DOZEN COOKIES

---

2 cups [165 g] hazelnut meal or flour

1 cup [200 g] packed jaggery or muscovado sugar

1½ tsp baking powder

½ tsp baking soda

½ tsp freshly ground black pepper

¼ tsp fine sea salt

1 large egg, lightly beaten

2 Tbsp unsalted butter, melted

1 tsp hazelnut extract or vanilla extract

½ cup [75 g] chopped bittersweet chocolate [70% cacao]

⅓ cup [55 g] chopped crystallized ginger

In a large bowl, whisk together the hazelnut meal, jaggery, baking powder, baking soda, black pepper, and salt. Add the egg, melted butter, hazelnut extract, chocolate, and ginger and stir with a large wooden spoon until the dough comes together. Grease your hands with a little oil to prevent the dough from sticking. Divide the dough into twelve equal parts and shape them into balls. Flatten them into 2 in [5 cm] rounds. Place the rounds on a baking sheet lined with parchment paper. Wrap the entire baking sheet tightly in plastic wrap and place in the freezer for at least 10 minutes, and preferably 2 hours.

To bake the cookies, preheat the oven to 350°F [180°C]. Line a second baking sheet with parchment paper. Remove the baking sheet from the freezer and put half the rounds of dough on the second sheet. Spread out the rounds on both baking sheets and refrigerate one of them. Bake one batch of cookies at a time until golden brown, 12 to 15 minutes. Cool completely on wire racks. Store the cookies in an airtight container at room temperature for up to 4 days.

THE APPROACH Black pepper and ginger add a kick of spicy heat, which intensifies the taste of the chocolate. If you want these even spicier, double the amount of pepper. The hazelnut extract amps up the hazelnut flavor of the nut meal. The end result is a cookie that's irresistible.

Sweet Potato Bebinca

Bebinca is the ultimate Goan dessert, an egg and coconut milk pudding, which can be made in several ways. My grandmother Lucy made one type that's called "mock bebinca," flavored with mashed sweet potatoes and scented with freshly grated nutmeg. I always make this recipe for Thanksgiving, but it's really a year-round treat.

MAKES 8 TO 9 SERVINGS (ONE 9 IN [23 CM] *BEBINCA*)

2 to 3 large sweet potatoes (1¼ lb [565 g] total)

6 Tbsp [85 g] butter, melted, plus more for the baking pan

6 large eggs

1 cup [200 g] jaggery or muscovado sugar

¼ cup [60 ml] maple syrup

1 tsp freshly grated nutmeg

½ tsp ground turmeric

¼ tsp fine sea salt

One 13½ oz [400 ml] can full-fat coconut milk

1 cup [140 g] all-purpose flour

Preheat the oven to 400°F [200°C]. Rinse the sweet potatoes to remove any dirt, pat them dry with paper towels, and poke several holes in them with a fork for the steam to escape. Put the potatoes in a baking dish or on baking sheet lined with aluminum foil. Roast until completely tender, 35 to 45 minutes. Cool completely before handling. Peel the sweet potatoes, discard the skins, and purée the flesh in a food processor. Measure out 1⅔ cups [400 g] and set aside, saving the rest for another purpose. (The sweet potatoes may be roasted 1 day ahead and stored in an airtight container in the refrigerator.) Reduce the oven temperature to 350°F [180°C].

Line the bottom of a 9 in [23 cm] round baking pan with 2 in [5 cm] sides with parchment paper and grease lightly with butter. Put the pan on a baking sheet. In a large bowl, whisk together the cooled roasted sweet potato purée, eggs, jaggery, maple syrup, 6 Tbsp [85 g] butter, nutmeg, turmeric, and salt until smooth. Add the coconut milk and flour and whisk until the mixture is smooth, with no visible streaks of flour.

Continued

THE APPROACH I use sweet potato varieties with orange flesh (such as Garnet and Jewel) when making this dessert. The turmeric bumps up the orange tones. (It works in pumpkin and sweet potato pie fillings for the same reason.) Freshly grated nutmeg adds a delicate but unmistakably sweet scent.

Pour the batter into the prepared cake pan and put the pan, still on the baking sheet, in the oven. Bake for 55 to 60 minutes, rotating the baking sheet halfway through. The pudding should be firm to the touch in the center and light golden brown around the edges. Remove from the oven, and cool completely in the pan on a wire rack. Wrap the pan with plastic wrap and refrigerate for at least 6 hours, and preferably overnight, to set.

Once the *bebinca* has set, run a sharp knife around the sides of the pan, flip the pan onto a baking sheet lined with parchment paper, and tap gently to release. Peel the parchment off the top. Invert onto a serving dish, and peel off the second sheet of parchment paper.

To serve, with a sharp, serrated knife, cut the chilled *bebinca* into wedges. Store the leftover *bebinca*, wrapped in plastic wrap, in an airtight container in the refrigerator for up to 1 week.

Apple Masala Chai Cake

I first made this cake several years ago when I started my blog, *A Brown Table*. It's rustic, with tender apples, and requires nothing more than a dusting of confectioners' sugar to finish it off. Because I call it a masala chai cake, it must, of course, have some tea in it; I grind Darjeeling leaves into the flour.

MAKES 8 TO 9 SERVINGS (ONE 9-IN [23-CM] CAKE)

¾ cup [165 g] unsalted butter, at room temperature, cubed, plus more to grease the cake pan

2 Tbsp Darjeeling tea leaves

2 cups [280 g] all-purpose flour

2 tsp baking powder

¼ tsp baking soda

1½ tsp Chai Masala (page 264)

¼ tsp fine sea salt

2 large Fuji or Granny Smith apples, cored, peeled, and diced

1 cup [200 g] packed brown sugar

4 large eggs, at room temperature

½ cup [60 g] confectioners' sugar

Grease a 9 in [23 cm] round baking pan with butter and line the bottom with parchment paper. Preheat the oven to 350°F [180°C].

Grind the tea leaves to a fine powder with a mortar and pestle. In a large bowl, whisk together the ground tea leaves, flour, baking powder, baking soda, chai masala, and salt. Put the apples in a medium bowl, and toss with 2 Tbsp of the whisked flour mixture, to coat.

In the bowl of a stand mixer fitted with the paddle attachment, cream the ¾ cup [165 g] butter and brown sugar on medium-high speed until light and fluffy, 2 to 3 minutes. Add the eggs, one at a time, beating after each addition. Lower the speed to medium-low, add the flour mixture, and beat until there are no more streaks of flour visible, 1 to 1½ minutes. Remove the bowl from the stand mixer and fold in the apples.

Continued

THE APPROACH Grinding the tea leaves before they go into the cake batter helps infuse the cake with their flavor. While the cake bakes, the baking soda reacts with the tannins in the tea to reduce any bitterness. This is a cake with lots of flavor for minimal effort, but be sure to use a fresh batch of chai masala.

Transfer the batter to the prepared pan and level it with an offset spatula. Bake for 55 to 60 minutes, rotating the pan halfway through baking, until the cake is golden brown, firm to the touch, and a skewer inserted into the center comes out clean. Cool in the pan on a wire rack for 5 minutes. Run a knife around the inside of the pan to release the cake. Transfer to a wire rack and cool completely. Before serving, dust the cake with confectioners' sugar. The cake will keep for 2 to 3 days at room temperature, in an airtight container lined with a clean kitchen towel to absorb any moisture.

Date and Tamarind Loaf

The inspiration for this cake is a sweet chutney made from dates and tamarind, which is commonly served as a dipping sauce with samosas and other fried snacks. I often dust this cake with confectioners' sugar or drizzle it with a little Kefir Crème Fraîche (page 260).

MAKES 8 TO 9 SERVINGS (ONE 8½ IN [21.5 CM] LOAF)

3¼ oz [90 g] sour tamarind pulp or paste

1 cup [240 ml] boiling water

2 cups [280 g] all-purpose flour

2 tsp ground ginger

½ tsp freshly ground black pepper

1½ tsp baking powder

½ tsp baking soda

¼ tsp fine sea salt

16 pitted Medjool dates, finely chopped

½ cup [60 g] chopped walnuts, plus 6 walnut halves

¾ cup [180 ml] plus 1 tsp extra-virgin olive oil

¾ cup [150 g] packed jaggery or muscovado sugar

2 large eggs, at room temperature

1 cup [120 g] confectioners' sugar

Put the tamarind in a medium heat-proof bowl and add the boiling water, pressing down on the tamarind with a spoon so it's covered with water. Cover with plastic wrap and let sit for at least 1 hour. Massage and squeeze the pulp to soften it, and press through a fine-mesh strainer suspended over a bowl, discarding the solids in the strainer. Measure out 1 cup [240 g] pulp for this recipe. Reserve 2 Tbsp of the pulp in a small bowl to prepare the glaze.

Preheat the oven to 350°F [180°C]. Grease an 8½ by 4½ in [21.5 by 11 cm] loaf pan with butter and line the bottom with parchment paper.

In a large bowl, whisk together the flour, ginger, pepper, baking powder, baking soda, and salt. Put the dates in a small bowl. Add the walnuts and 2 Tbsp of the whisked dry ingredients and toss to coat evenly.

Combine the ¾ cup [180 ml] olive oil and jaggery in a blender and pulse on high speed for a few seconds until completely emulsified. Add one egg and pulse for 3 to 4 seconds, until combined. Repeat with the remaining egg.

THE APPROACH A high-speed blender is a marvelous tool to use for olive oil cakes because it can quickly whip air and emulsify the liquids in the batter to create a delicate cake crumb. This cake is first spiced with ginger and black pepper and sweetened with jaggery, adding contrast to the tamarind and dates in the batter, and then finally drizzled with a tamarind glaze to add a pop of fruitiness. I prefer to use the sour tamarind found in the Asian grocery stores rather than the sweeter Mexican variety because its stronger flavor comes through better in baking.

Make a well in the center of the dry ingredients in the bowl, and pour the egg mixture into the well. Whisk the dry ingredients into the egg mixture and continue whisking until there are no visible flecks of flour. Then fold in the dates and walnuts.

Spoon the batter into the prepared loaf pan. Arrange the walnuts halves in a straight line down the center of the loaf. Bake for 55 to 60 minutes, rotating the pan halfway through baking, until firm to the touch in the center and a skewer comes out clean. Cool in the pan on a wire rack for about 10 minutes, and run a knife around the inside of the pan to release the cake. Remove from the pan and transfer to a wire rack to cool completely.

Add the remaining 1 tsp of olive oil to the small bowl containing the reserved tamarind. Sift in the confectioners' sugar and whisk until completely smooth. Pour the glaze over the cooled loaf and let it sit for 1 hour to set before serving.

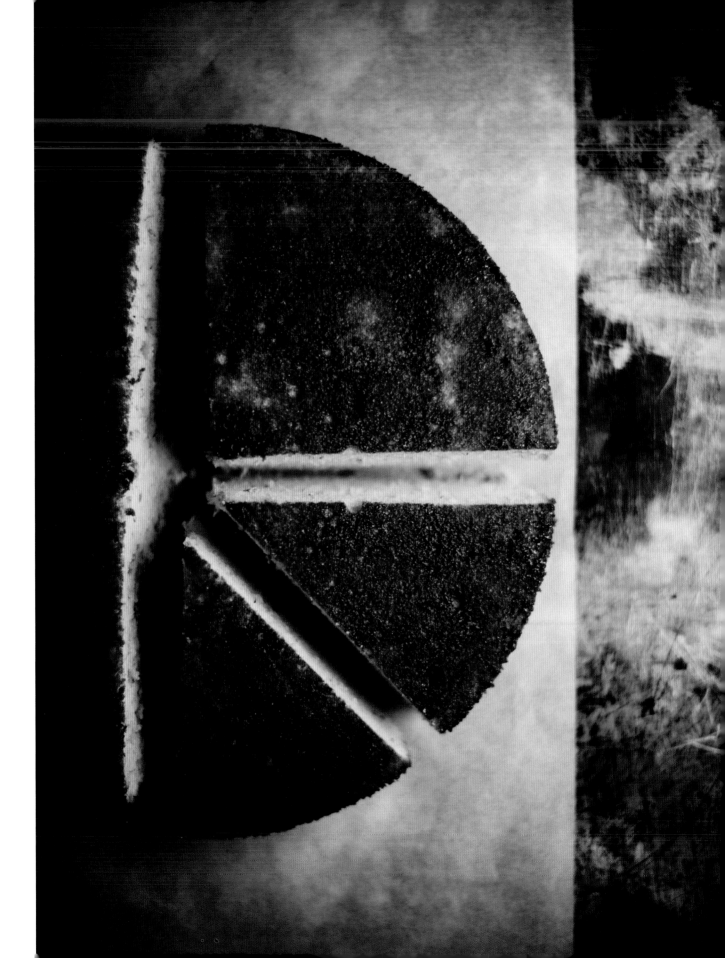

Elderflower and Ghee Cake

In India, especially in the north, ghee is used to cook almost everything—including desserts. We even like to fry nuts and raisins in ghee to garnish *kheer* (a rice pudding). Elderflower cordial adds a floral note to this highly aromatic cake. Serve with a dollop of sweetened crème fraîche (page 200) and fresh berries.

MAKES 8 TO 9 SERVINGS (ONE 9 IN [23 CM] CAKE)

1 cup [200 g] Ghee (page 268), melted, plus more to grease the pan

3 Tbsp jaggery or muscovado sugar

2 cups [280 g] all-purpose flour

2 tsp baking powder

½ tsp fine sea salt

1 cup [200 g] sugar

4 large eggs, at room temperature

½ cup [120 ml] 2 percent milk, at room temperature

½ cup [120 ml] elderflower cordial

Preheat the oven to 350°F [180°C]. Grease a 9 in [23 cm] round cake pan with a little melted ghee and line with parchment paper. Brush the parchment paper with a little more ghee. Sprinkle the jaggery on the bottom and sides of the pan, rotating the pan to coat evenly.

In a medium bowl, whisk together the flour, baking powder, and salt. In a large bowl, whisk together the 1 cup [200 g] ghee and sugar until you get a smooth slurry. Whisk in the eggs, one at a time, until well combined. Add half the dry ingredients and whisk until smooth. Whisk in all of the milk, and then the remaining dry ingredients, whisking until the batter is smooth and there are no visible streaks of flour. Transfer the batter to the prepared pan and level the surface with a small offset spatula.

Bake for 45 to 50 minutes, rotating the pan halfway through baking. Remove the cake from the oven and cool in the pan on a wire rack for 5 minutes. Run a knife around the inside of the pan to release the sides of the cake. Invert the cake onto a serving plate, gently tapping the pan to release the bottom. Let the cake cool for another 5 minutes, and then carefully peel off the parchment paper. Cool to room temperature. Brush the cake generously with the elderflower cordial and let sit for another 10 minutes to absorb the liquid before serving. Store leftover cake, wrapped in parchment paper and aluminum foil, for up to 4 days at room temperature.

THE APPROACH Ghee is prepared by boiling off the water in butter and caramelizing the milk solids. The fat and the jaggery flavor the cake as it bakes. If you want to make the cake a little boozy, you can replace the cordial with an elderflower liqueur, such as St-Germain. Alternatively, add ½ tsp ground cardamom to the batter.

Upside-Down Orange and Fennel Cornmeal Cake

The farmers' market at Lake Merritt, in Oakland, is filled with beautiful oranges during the winter and early spring. You'll find Valencias, blood oranges, navel oranges, satsumas, and more. What better way to showcase those gorgeous oranges than in this upside-down cake, scented with fennel and lightly caramelized.

When making cakes with a coarse meal or flour, such as cornmeal, I use a trick I learned from my grandmother: I let the cake batter sit overnight in the refrigerator, so it absorbs as much liquid as possible. It gives the cake a very tender crumb.

MAKES 12 SERVINGS (ONE 12 IN [30.5 CM] CAKE)

1½ cups plus 1 Tbsp [345 g] unsalted butter, at room temperature, plus 4 Tbsp [55 g], melted, to grease the baking pan

1 tsp fennel seeds

3 Tbsp plus 1½ cups [300 g] sugar

2 blood oranges, unpeeled

1 Valencia orange, unpeeled

2 cups [280 g] fine cornmeal

2 cups [280 g] all-purpose flour or whole-wheat pastry flour

1 Tbsp baking powder

1 Tbsp grated orange zest

1 tsp ground fennel

¼ tsp fine sea salt

6 large eggs, at room temperature

¾ cup [180 ml] fresh tangerine or orange juice (any type of orange)

Using a pastry brush, liberally grease a 12 in [30.5 cm] round cake pan with half the melted butter. Line the pan with a parchment round and brush the paper with the remaining melted butter. Sprinkle the whole fennel seeds and 3 Tbsp of the sugar over the bottom of the pan. Using a sharp knife or mandoline, slice the oranges ⅛ in [4 mm] thick. Arrange the orange slices over the sugar and fennel seeds, covering as much surface area as you can.

In a large bowl, whisk together the cornmeal, flour, baking powder, orange zest, ground fennel, and salt. In the bowl of a stand mixer fitted with the paddle attachment, cream the remaining 1½ cups plus 1 Tbsp [345 g] butter

Continued

THE APPROACH Upside-down cakes have a lot of advantages. Because the orange slices, fennel seeds, and sugar are placed at the bottom of the pan, the heat of the pan caramelizes the sugars and toasts the fennel seeds. These flavors infuse the cake as it bakes. And the caramelized fruit adds a dimension of beauty and a layer of concentrated sweetness.

and remaining 1½ cups [300 g] sugar for 4 to 5 minutes on medium-high speed, until light and fluffy. Add the eggs, one at a time, beating after each addition. Lower the mixer speed to medium-low and add half the dry ingredients, beating until combined, 1 to 1½ minutes. Beat in the tangerine juice, and then the remaining dry ingredients, and beat until well combined and there are no visible streaks of flour. Transfer the batter to the prepared pan. Cover the surface of the batter with plastic wrap and refrigerate for at least 8 hours, and preferably overnight.

When ready to bake, preheat the oven to 350°F [180°C]. Bake the cake for 55 to 60 minutes, rotating the pan halfway through baking, until the center is firm, yet spongy, and a skewer inserted into the center comes out clean.

Place the pan on a wire rack and cool for 10 minutes. Run a knife around the inside of the pan to loosen the cake, and invert the cake onto a plate. Let cool for another 10 to 12 minutes, and then gently tap the bottom of the pan to unmold the cake. Peel off the parchment paper and cool completely. To serve, cut the cake with a sharp, serrated knife.

Rum-Soaked Raisin Caramel Cake

Fruit cake is a matter of pride for many Indian Catholics. In fact, I don't think I've ever been to a wedding or spent a Christmas where people didn't serve it. As soon as Christmas ends in December, people start soaking their raisins in large jars of Old Monk rum (an Indian brand of spiced rum available in America) for the following Christmas. This is my grandmother's recipe, with a few modifications.

MAKES 12 TO 14 SERVINGS (ONE 9 CUP [2.1 L] BUNDT CAKE)

1½ cups [210 g] mixed raisins

1½ cups [360 ml] spiced rum

1 Tbsp unsalted butter, melted, plus 1 cup [220 g] at room temperature

3½ cups plus 2 Tbsp [715 g] sugar

½ cup [120 ml] water

¼ tsp cream of tartar

3½ cups plus 2 Tbsp [500 g] all-purpose flour

1½ tsp baking powder

½ tsp fine sea salt

½ cup [110 g] chopped candied ginger

⅔ cup [100 g] chopped dried apricots or pineapples

⅓ cup [50 g] chopped raw cashews

5 large eggs, at room temperature

Put the raisins in a 6½ cup [1.5 L] clean, sterilized jar with a lid or a large resealable plastic bag. Warm the rum in a small saucepan over low heat until it just starts to simmer, and pour the rum over the raisins. Close the bag or seal the jar. Leave in a cool and dark place for at least 12 hours and up to 1 month. Shake the jar or bag occasionally to redistribute the raisins.

Preheat the oven to 300°F [150°C]. Brush a 9 cup [2.1 L] Bundt pan with 1 Tbsp of melted butter, taking care to reach all the folds of the pan. Sprinkle 2 Tbsp of sugar inside the pan and shake to coat evenly.

Heat 1 cup [200 g] of the sugar, ¼ cup [60 ml] water, and the cream of tartar in a small, heavy-bottomed saucepan over medium-high heat, stirring to dissolve the sugar. Continue cooking, swirling the boiling sugar in the saucepan, until it turns a deep shade of brown, 8 to 10 minutes. Remove from the heat, stir in the remaining ¼ cup [60 ml] water to form a thick syrup, and let cool for about 30 minutes. If stiff, stir in 2 Tbsp of water.

THE APPROACH Start with a good-quality spiced rum you really enjoy, because it flavors the cake. Caramel lends both bittersweet notes and amber color. The darker you cook your sugar, the deeper the color will be.

In a large bowl, whisk together the flour, baking powder, and salt. Transfer ½ cup [70 g] to a medium bowl. Drain the rum from the soaked raisins into a small bowl and set aside. In another small bowl, toss the raisins with the ginger, apricots, cashews, and the ½ cup flour mixture, stirring to coat evenly.

In the bowl of a stand mixer fitted with the paddle attachment, cream the remaining 1 cup [220 g] butter and 2½ cups [500 g] of sugar on medium-high speed until light and fluffy, 3 to 4 minutes. Reduce the mixer speed to low and slowly pour the warm caramel down the side of the mixer bowl in a thin stream. Beat until blended. Add the eggs, one at a time, beating after each addition until combined; do not overbeat. Add the dry ingredients in two batches, beating after each addition until no visible streaks of flour remain. Remove the bowl from the stand mixer and fold in the flour-coated dried fruits and nuts.

Transfer the batter to the prepared cake pan and bake for about 2½ to 3 hours, rotating the pan once during baking. The cake is done when a skewer inserted into the middle of the cake comes out clean, or when the internal temperature is 210°F [99°C]. Remove the cake from the oven and cool in the pan on a wire rack for 5 minutes. Check to see if the edges of the cake are pulling away from the sides of the pan. If not, use a butter knife to nudge the cake a little. Invert the cake, still in the pan, onto the rack and let stand for 5 to 10 minutes. To release the cake, tap the sides and top of the pan gently and remove. After 15 minutes, brush the cake with the reserved soaking rum. Cool completely before serving. The cake will keep, tightly wrapped in plastic wrap, for up to 1 week at room temperature, and up to 3 weeks in the refrigerator. (You may want to drizzle the cake with a little more rum before serving.)

CHAPTER 8: Sips

In this chapter, I've included recipes for some of my favorite drinks, with and without alcohol. When making a drink, decide whether you're going to serve it with food; or at the end of a meal, as a stand-in for dessert; or to give yourself a boost during the day. Yogurt-based drinks such as lassis (page 232) aid with digestion and calm the body at the end of a spicy meal. Other drinks, like cardamom-infused iced coffee (page 239), energize and stimulate the senses.

My grandmother had a tradition of ending every large family dinner or celebration with a glass of port wine, which was also the drink of choice at Catholic weddings in India, to accompany the wedding cake. I prefer a glass of red or white with a meal, and sometimes a flute of Champagne.

Alcohol is a wonderful solvent. For example, you can use gin to extract the aromas and flavors of pineapple and serrano chiles (page 243). And brandy will do the same for rainbow peppercorns and cardamom, to produce a delicious Bellini (page 240).

A blender and a mortar and pestle are all you need to make most of the drinks in this chapter. And time. Read through the recipe you've chosen carefully, in case you need to make a crucial extract or concentrate hours or even days before serving.

Lemonade Two Ways

Come summer we drink ridiculous amounts of lemonade. Starting with a lemon simple syrup gives you the flexibility to take this lemonade in two different directions: a floral orange blossom lemonade or one scented with toasted cumin. If you're like me and love fizzy lemonades, dilute the concentrate with chilled club soda.

Orange Blossom Lemonade

MAKES 6 SERVINGS

Lemon Simple Syrup

1 cup [200 g] sugar

1 cup [240 ml] water

1 cup [240 ml] fresh lemon juice

2 Tbsp orange blossom water

3 cups [720 ml] chilled club soda or water

Fresh baby mint leaves or orange blossoms
    (or both) for garnish (optional)

To make the lemon simple syrup: In a medium saucepan, combine the sugar and water and bring to a simmer over medium-high heat, stirring until the sugar dissolves. Remove from the heat and cool to room temperature. Stir in the lemon juice.

To finish the lemonade, stir the orange blossom water into the lemon simple syrup to form a concentrate. To serve, fill six tall glasses with ice. Pour 4 oz [120 ml] of the lemon syrup–orange blossom concentrate into each glass, top with 4 oz [120 ml] of the club soda or chilled water, and stir. Garnish with the mint leaves or orange blossoms, or both, if desired. Store any leftover concentrate in an airtight container in the refrigerator for up to 1 week.

Continued

THE APPROACH The lemon syrup gives you the ultimate flexibility. If you're in the mood for something that's refreshing and lightly fragrant, go for the lemonade made with the orange blossom water, as you'll love its sweet floral scent. The toasted cumin version offers something deeper and earthier: a drink with hints of warm spice and subtle smokiness.

Toasted Cumin Lemonade

MAKES 6 SERVINGS

Lemon Simple Syrup (see page 225)

1½ Tbsp cumin seeds

3 cups [720 ml] chilled club soda or water

Lemon slices or fresh baby mint leaves (or both) for garnish (optional)

Make the simple syrup and set aside. Heat a small, dry skillet over high heat and add the cumin seeds. Toast the seeds until fragrant, swirling the seeds occasionally so they toast evenly, 30 to 45 seconds. Transfer the hot seeds to a mortar and pestle or a spice grinder and grind to a fine powder. Quickly add the toasted cumin to the simple syrup. Stir and let sit, covered, for 5 minutes.

To serve, fill six tall glasses with ice. Pour 4 oz [120 ml] of the cumin-and-lemon-flavored syrup into each glass, top with 4 oz [120 ml] of the club soda or chilled water, and stir. Garnish with the lemon slices or mint leaves, or both, if desired. Store any leftover syrup in an airtight container in the refrigerator for up to 1 week.

Ginger and Tamarind Refresher

While it is not uncommon to find ginger blended into limeades, lemonades, and fresh sugarcane juice in India, it also pairs nicely with tamarind. Serve cold and give it a good stir before drinking.

This recipe is made with tamarind pulp, which contains large seeds that you will need to remove. Avoid the temptation to use concentrates. They're more convenient because they don't have seeds, but they don't taste nearly as fresh.

MAKES 8 SERVINGS

2½ cups [600 ml] water

2½ oz [70 g] sour tamarind pulp or paste

8 oz [225 g] fresh ginger, preferably young

1 cup [200 g] sugar

One 1 L bottle chilled club soda or 4 cups [960 ml] chilled water

Bring 1½ cups [360 ml] of the water to a boil. Put the tamarind pulp in a heat-proof nonreactive bowl, and cover with the boiling water. Cover and let sit for about 1 hour, until the pulp has become soft and mushy. Using a small potato masher or clean hands, massage and squeeze the block to soften the pulp. Strain through a fine-mesh strainer suspended over a medium bowl, pressing the pulp through the strainer with a large spoon. Discard the seeds and other solids left behind. Refrigerate the tamarind extract in an airtight container in the refrigerator until ready to use, for up to 4 days.

Rinse the ginger and gently scrub to remove any traces of dirt. If the ginger is young, with a thin skin, leave the skin on. Otherwise, peel. Cut into thin slices. In a medium saucepan, combine the ginger, sugar, and remaining 1 cup [240 ml] water. Bring to a boil over medium-high heat and immediately remove the saucepan from the heat. Cover and steep for 10 minutes. Strain the ginger simple syrup through a fine-mesh strainer and discard the ginger.

In a large pitcher, mix the tamarind extract and the ginger simple syrup together. Fill eight tall glasses with ice. Pour 4 oz [120 ml] of the tamarind-ginger syrup into each glass, top with 4 oz [120 ml] of the club soda or chilled water, and stir. Store any remaining tamarind-ginger syrup in an airtight container in the refrigerator for up to 1 week.

THE APPROACH This rejuvenating drink combines the mild heat of young ginger and the sourness of tamarind. It's wonderful during the warmer months. Young ginger requires no peeling before use because its outer skin is so thin. I recommend using South Asian tamarind, which is a lot more sour than the Mexican variety. Look for it in Asian and Indian markets.

Rhubarb, Cardamom, and Rose Water Sharbat

A *sharbat* is a sweet, sometimes floral, fruit drink common in India, the Middle East, and parts of Africa. (The word is derived from Persian.) They are usually served chilled. This *sharbat* was inspired by some leftover rhubarb purée from a dessert I'd created for my column in the *San Francisco Chronicle*. The purée's vibrant shade of red and irresistible aromas from cardamom and rose water convinced me it would make a wonderful base for a *sharbat*.

MAKES 4 SERVINGS

1¼ lb [570 g] rhubarb stalks

Seeds from 5 green cardamom pods, crushed

1 cup [200 g] sugar

1 cup [240 ml] water

½ tsp rose water

2 cups [480 ml] chilled water for serving

Preheat the oven to 375°F [190°C]. Trim and discard the ends of the rhubarb stalks and cut the stalks crosswise into 1 in [2.5 cm] pieces. Transfer the rhubarb to a baking sheet. Sprinkle the rhubarb with the cardamom, and then with ½ cup [100 g] of the sugar. Toss to coat evenly. Roast the rhubarb until the sugar caramelizes and starts to turn dark brown, the rhubarb softens, and the juices bubble, 12 to 15 minutes. Remove the pan from the oven and cool the rhubarb for about 10 minutes. Using a silicone spatula, scrape the rhubarb into a medium container (4½ cup [1 L] capacity or larger is ideal) with an airtight lid. Set aside, uncovered.

Meanwhile, prepare the simple syrup. In a small saucepan, combine the remaining ½ cup [100 g] sugar and the 1 cup [240 ml] water and bring to a rolling boil over medium-high heat. Remove from the heat and pour over the rhubarb mixture. Stir in the rose water, cover the container, and refrigerate for at least 6 hours, and preferably overnight. Line a fine-mesh strainer with several layers of cheesecloth and strain the rhubarb concentrate into a bowl, pressing with a wooden spoon to release as much liquid as possible from the fruit.

To serve, fill four tall glasses with ice. Pour 4 oz [120 ml] of the rhubarb concentrate into each glass, top with 4 oz [120 ml] of the chilled water, and stir. Store any leftover concentrate in an airtight container in the refrigerator for up to 1 week.

THE APPROACH Roasting rhubarb with sugar and cardamom breaks down the oxalic acid in the rhubarb, introduces mild notes of caramel, and intensifies the red color of the fruit. Because rose water is highly aromatic and volatile, I add it toward the end so it retains its potency.

Salted Tarragon Lassi

Lassis are the perfect summer drink when you want to cool off. Indian restaurants have popularized sweet mango lassis, but salted lassi, or *chaas*, are equally worthy. This one, with fresh tarragon, makes a soothing, creamy impression as you sip.

MAKES 2 SERVINGS

½ tsp cumin seeds

1 cup [240 g] full-fat plain yogurt

1 cup [240 ml] chilled water

¼ cup [3 g] packed fresh tarragon leaves

½ tsp sea salt

Heat a small, dry skillet over high heat and add the cumin seeds. Toast the seeds until fragrant, swirling the seeds occasionally so they toast evenly, 30 to 45 seconds. Transfer the seeds to a mortar and pestle or a spice grinder and grind to a coarse powder.

In a blender, combine the yogurt, water, tarragon, and salt and blend until smooth. Taste and adjust seasoning if needed. Divide between two glasses and garnish with the ground toasted cumin. Serve cold.

THE APPROACH You can make a salted lassi with almost any fresh herb. In addition to tarragon, I enjoy them with basil and cilantro, and I especially like to use members of the mint family. You can also add a serrano chile and blend it with the yogurt. Remove the seeds first, though, if you'd like to tamp down the heat. The final consistency of a lassi should not be too thick, which is why it's traditionally made with water, rather than milk. For the same reason, you should avoid using Greek yogurt.

Saffron and Cardamom Milk

When I was a kid, my mom would send me off to buy yogurt from our local dairy. Even in a large metropolis like Bombay, back in the 1990s there were no supermarkets, just local vendors who owned small specialty food stores. I didn't enjoy making that trek, but I loved the glass of sweet and creamy spiced almond milk the shopkeeper would give me. And I liked to watch him cut chunks from the yogurt. It resembled a big, soft, pudding, which he kept in a large metallic vessel.

MAKES 2 SERVINGS

2 cups [280 g] whole raw almonds

2 cups [480 ml] water

2 cups [480 ml] chilled whole milk

2 Tbsp honey or 3 Tbsp maple syrup, or more as needed

Seeds from 3 green cardamom pods, crushed

½ tsp saffron strands, plus 6 to 8 more strands for garnish

In a small bowl, combine the almonds and the water. Let sit, covered, overnight. Drain off the water and rub the skins off the almonds, if desired. (If you want to remove them completely, see The Approach.) Transfer the almonds to a blender and add the milk, honey, cardamom seeds, and ½ tsp saffron strands. Pulse until smooth. Taste and add more honey if you want it sweeter. Strain the milk through a strainer if you wish. To serve, fill two tall glasses with ice and divide the nut milk between them. Garnish each glass with 3 or 4 saffron strands.

THE APPROACH Soaking nuts in water makes them creamier and allows their skins to slough off more easily. To remove the skins completely, drain the soaked nuts and transfer to a heat-proof bowl. Cover with 2 cups [480 ml] boiling water and let sit for 4 minutes. Drain well, and rub off the skins.

The ground almonds help thicken the milk and add a certain sweetness, too. Cardamom can act as a cooling agent in desserts and beverages, which should come as no surprise because it's especially popular in countries where summers are extremely hot. A tiny bit of saffron goes a long way in this drink. To further heighten the drink's floral character, add a drop or two of rose water and garnish with fresh rose petals.

Spiced Mango Milkshake

My grandfather's ancestral home in Goa had two large mango trees out back. Every summer, the entire family would spend a few weeks there together, right when the trees were laden with ripe, juicy, sweet mangoes. Indian mangoes are best eaten raw or paired with just a few ingredients. I love Alphonso mangoes the best. They're less fibrous and have no discernible chalkiness. If you can't find them, use Champagne mangoes instead.

MAKES 4 SERVINGS

2 ripe mangoes (8½ oz [480 g] each)

½ tsp ground cinnamon

Seeds from 1 green cardamom pod, crushed

2 Tbsp maple syrup, or more as needed

2 cups [480 ml] chilled whole milk or almond milk

½ cup [70 g] unsalted raw cashews

A few strands of saffron for garnish (optional)

Peel the mangoes, discard the pits, and dice the pulp. Transfer to a blender and add the remaining ingredients, except for the saffron. Pulse on high speed until well combined and smooth. Taste and add more maple syrup if you want a sweeter drink.

To serve, put some crushed ice in each of four glasses. Pour in the milkshake, and garnish with the saffron, if desired.

THE APPROACH This milkshake's success depends on the mangoes; they should be ripe. When you hold a ripe mango close to your nose and take a whiff, it will be extremely fragrant. Cardamom and cinnamon are highly aromatic spices with cooling and warming effects on the palate and they work well with mangoes and other sweet fruit. Cashews, when blended into a drink, make it richer and creamier.

Cardamom Iced Coffee with Coconut Milk

Here's an easy way to upgrade your glass of iced coffee with minimal effort. Sweeten, if desired.

MAKES 1 SERVING

Seeds from 1 green cardamom pod, crushed

1 cup [120 ml] strong brewed coffee, chilled

2 oz [60 ml] coconut milk

Grind the cardamom seeds with a mortar and pestle or a spice grinder. Transfer to a cocktail shaker and add the coffee. Shake for a few seconds. Fill a tall glass with ice and pour in the coffee. Drizzle in the coconut milk, and serve immediately.

THE APPROACH You could also brew the coffee with the cardamom by adding the ground seeds to your ground beans. The hot water will draw out more of the essential and aromatic oils of the spice. Green cardamom is highly aromatic, and grinding the seeds down to a fine powder allows them to disperse easily into the drink, adding its characteristic floral flavor in seconds.

Bellini with Cardamom and Peppercorns

When I host brunches for family and friends, I tend to serve Indian-inspired versions of my favorite Champagne-based drinks, like this Bellini, whose flavors remind me of Bombay.

MAKES 4 SERVINGS

Infused Peaches

4 ripe yellow peaches (1¼ lb [570 g] total), peeled, pitted, and quartered

½ cup [120 ml] brandy

½ tsp rainbow peppercorns

4 whole green cardamom pods

¼ cup [50 g] jaggery

One 750 ml bottle chilled Rosé Champagne for serving

To make the peaches: In a blender, combine 2 of the peaches with the brandy and pulse until puréed. Transfer to a clean canning jar with a tight-fitting lid. Gently crack the peppercorns and the whole cardamom pods with a mortar and pestle and toss them into the jar. Add the remaining 2 peaches to the jar. Seal and shake the jar a few times; refrigerate overnight.

To serve, crush the jaggery to a fine powder (see page 253) and put 1 Tbsp in the bottom of each of four Champagne flutes. Fish out 1 slice of peach and 1 or 2 peppercorns from the jar, and place on top of the jaggery in each flute and add ¼ cup [60 ml] of the peach purée. Top off with Champagne and serve immediately.

THE APPROACH Lightly cracking the peppercorns and bruising the cardamom before they steep in the brandy makes the extraction process more effective. I've chosen jaggery as my sweetener here because it gives the Bellini an earthy minerality. Instead of the rainbow peppercorns, you can use Tellicherry black peppercorns, which are not as hot as regular black peppercorns but have a stronger fragrance.

Pineapple Serrano Gin

This sunny and fruity cocktail goes with any meal and is one of the most exciting drinks I serve my guests in summer. Because the serrano infusion is mild, you get the flavor of the chiles along with the piney notes from the gin, but no jolt of chile heat.

MAKES 6 SERVINGS

1 ripe pineapple (about 1½ lb [680 g])

2 serrano chiles, plus 1, thinly sliced, for garnish (optional)

1 cup [240 ml] gin

½ cup [100 g] sugar

1½ cups [360 ml] chilled water

Twist and then cut off the top of the pineapple, and cut off the stem end (discard both). Holding the pineapple in a vertical position, with a sharp knife, cut off the prickly skin with long, downward strokes. Using a small paring knife, remove any eyes (the brown hard, spiny spots). Cut 1 lb [455 g] of the pineapple into rough chunks and transfer to a blender. (Store any leftover pineapple, covered, in the refrigerator for another use.) Pulse the pineapple until puréed and transfer to a clean 1 qt [960 ml] glass jar with a tight-fitting lid. Slit open the 2 whole serrano chiles lengthwise and add them to the pineapple. Pour in the gin and add the sugar. Seal the jar and shake a few times to dissolve the sugar. Refrigerate for 1 to 2 days to allow the alcohol to extract the flavors.

When ready to enjoy, line a strainer with three or four layers of cheesecloth and dampen them. Set the strainer over another jar or a large measuring cup and strain the pineapple serrano gin concentrate, squeezing the cheesecloth to release any liquid still trapped in the pulp. To serve, fill six tall glasses with ice. Pour ½ cup [120 ml] of the concentrate into each glass, top with ¼ cup [60 ml] of the chilled water, and stir. Garnish with a few slices of serrano chile. (Store any unused concentrate in a jar, tightly covered, in the refrigerator for up to 1 week.)

THE APPROACH Puréeing the pineapple before it's added to the gin helps extract the fruit's tropical flavors and also its gorgeous bright-yellow pigments. Because I don't want this drink to be peppery hot, I simply slit open the serrano chiles lengthwise and allow them to steep in the gin along with the fruit, rather than puréeing the chiles with the pineapple. The result is a very subtle hit of chile with each sip. Because gin is prepared by infusing alcohol with juniper berries and a variety of spices (which varies by manufacturer), play around with different brands to find the one that works best for you.

Pomegranate Moscow Mule

I encountered my first Moscow mule at Hamburger Mary's, a Cincinnati bar I frequented with my graduate school friends on weekends. I loved their version of the drink, with fresh ginger and lime-flavored vodka. Over the years, I've made some modifications. This pomegranate version is one I turn to every fall. And it's always on my Thanksgiving menu.

MAKES 1 SERVING

¼ cup [60 ml] unflavored vodka

4 Tbsp [60 ml] fresh pomegranate juice

½ tsp pomegranate molasses

1 Tbsp [15 ml] fresh lime juice

1 Tbsp [15 ml] maple syrup

¾ cup [180 ml] good quality ginger beer

¼ tsp ground anardana

1 lime peel for garnish

Fill a copper mug with ice. Mix the vodka, pomegranate juice, molasses, lime juice, and maple syrup in a mixing glass and stir until well combined. Stir in the ginger beer and pour into the ice-filled mug. Garnish with the anardana and lime peel, and serve immediately.

THE APPROACH Pomegranates are a staple in most Mediterranean, Middle Eastern, and Indian diets. The bright ruby fruit encases jewel-like capsules, which contain a tiny burst of sweet and tart juice. The juice pairs especially well with the spicy ginger and fresh lime notes in the drink. I add a pinch of ground anardana (dried pomegranate seeds) to bump up the molasses flavor. You might be wondering whether it's important to serve this drink in a copper mug. You can surely do without it, but copper conducts temperature really well, and a cold mug adds a pleasantly shivery sensation as you sip your drink.

Caramelized Fig and Bourbon Iced Chai

Fresh figs, a good bourbon, and chai masala are three of my favorite "food groups," and this drink is my ode to that happy trio in one cocktail. I prepare the fresh fig extract in large jars when figs are in season and let them sit in my pantry. That way, I can make a bourbon iced chai whenever I like. Over time, the figs absorb the bourbon. Once I've depleted the extract, I cook the fruit left behind to make jam or fig butter.

MAKES 4 SERVINGS

Caramelized Fig and Bourbon Extract

10 oz [280 g] fresh figs, quartered

1 Tbsp sugar

2 cups [480 ml] bourbon

2 Tbsp [30 ml] maple syrup

Bourbon Iced Chai

4 black tea bags, such as orange pekoe or Darjeeling

1 tsp Chai Masala (page 264)

2 cups [480 ml] boiling water

Four 3 in [7.5 cm] strips lemon peel for garnish (optional)

To make the extract: Preheat the broiler. Put the figs on a baking sheet with a rim and sprinkle the sugar on top. Broil until the juices start to bubble and caramelize, 5 to 6 minutes. (Watch carefully so the figs do not burn.) Remove from the oven and transfer the fruit to a clean jar with a tight-fitting lid. Pour about ¾ cup [180 ml] of the bourbon over the baking sheet, scrape the pan gently with a wooden spoon to release any stuck bits of fig, and cover with aluminum foil. Let sit until any caramelized bits still stuck to the pan start to dissolve, 20 to 30 minutes. Tip the bourbon and loosened bits into the jar with the figs. Add the remaining 1¼ cups [300 ml] bourbon and the maple syrup. Mash the figs in the jar with a muddler, a small potato masher, or a wooden spoon. Cover with the lid and shake a few times. Refrigerate the extract for 1 week before using.

To make the bourbon iced chai: Chill four glasses. Put the tea bags and chai masala blend in a heat-proof bowl or a teapot. Cover with the boiling water and allow the tea and spices to steep for 5 to 6 minutes. Discard the tea bags. Pour the spiced tea into a large pitcher and stir in 2 cups [480 ml] of the fig and bourbon extract. Stir and taste, adjusting the sweetness with maple syrup, if necessary. Fill the chilled glasses with ice, pour in the iced chai, and garnish each one with a lemon peel.

THE APPROACH Because figs are rich in sugar, caramelizing them under the broiler burns the sugar and deepens the caramel flavors. The bourbon helps extract those flavors during steeping. This drink is the perfect example of the happy alchemy that occurs when the warmer flavors of the bourbon, caramelized figs, chai masala, and tea are served at a cooler temperature, over ice.

CHAPTER 9: Staples

I firmly believe that a person's wealth lies in his or her kitchen pantry, and by that, I mean the assortment of condiments that help transform a boring meal into one that's spectacular! The pantry is the cook's arsenal. It's where endless possibilities reside for adding flavor and texture to all kinds of dishes. Drizzle a little garlicky sesame oil (page 259) over your oven-roasted vegetables or season your fish or chicken with a little Garam Masala (page 263) before you cook them. There are so many different ways to bring a world of flavor to your food.

I picked up my appreciation for the power of the pantry from my parents. Their shelves and refrigerator doors were always filled with masalas (spice blends), pickled vegetables, condiments, and sauces. You could eat a boiled egg every day and never be bored because there was always a different way to flavor it.

Tamarind

Tamarind is a tropical fruit that's typically used in African, Asian, and Mexican cuisines. Some producers label tamarind "sour Asian" or "sweet Mexican," which refers to the stage at which the fruit was harvested. The longer the fruit ages, the sweeter it gets. I usually stick with the sour variety and then sweeten as needed.

Tamarind is available in four different forms: the whole fruit in the pods (top left); a wet, seedless cake of pulp, which some producers call "paste" (top right); a dried block of pulp with seeds (bottom left); and a liquid concentrate with a dark, molasseslike color and texture (bottom right). The dried pulp and the wet paste are basically the same thing. You can use either one for the recipes in this book. Avoid the liquid concentrate, though, because it's been cooked down, it doesn't taste the same. (I find it a little off.) Working with the fruit or the seedless cakes at home, it's very easy and requires only a short amount of time. If you buy the whole fruit in their pods, remove as much of the shell as you can and follow the instructions in the recipe for softening it in boiling water and straining the fruit, which will take care of any pieces of shell.

How to Prepare Tamarind

This is the method I use to extract tamarind paste. I typically extract once with hot water, but some cooks might also do a second extraction, which depends on how much pulp was extracted the first time.

MAKES 1¼ CUPS [300 ML/360 G]

8 to 12 whole tamarind fruit pods

or

1 cup or 9¼ oz [260 g] packed, seedless tamarind
    paste

2 cups [480 ml] boiling water

Remove and discard as much of the outer brittle shell on the fruit pods by cracking it gently with your fingers. Discard any large stringy fibers that might be present. Then place the extracted fruit in a heat-proof, non-reactive bowl. Alternatively, if you're working with the pre-cleaned seedless pulp, place it in a heat-proof, non-reactive bowl. Cover the pulp with the boiling water, stir, and let it sit for 1 hour at room temperature to soften. Press the pulp down using a small potato masher or massage the softened pulp with your fingers to release it. Pass the tamarind pulp through a fine-mesh sieve set over a bowl and press it as much as you can, using a large spoon to release as much fruit pulp as you can extract. Discard the material left behind in the sieve and use the extract to cook with. Tamarind extract will resemble a thick toffee-colored purée and can be stored in an airtight plastic container in the refrigerator for up to 1 week, or you can freeze it in resealable bags for up to 3 weeks.

Jaggery

Jaggery is an unrefined form of sugar obtained by evaporating either sugarcane juice or the juice of the date palm. It comes in various shades, from light to dark golden brown. It also comes in many forms, from blocks to granular jaggery, which is easier to measure when cooking. Blocks are soft enough, though, so that you can cut off as much as you need with a large knife. Transfer the chunk of jaggery to a resealable plastic bag and pound it gently with a rolling pin or a heavy pan to crush it. Because jaggery is an unrefined sweetener, it carries a lot of minerals and salts, which make it hygroscopic (it absorbs moisture from the air). So always store it in an airtight container.

Eggs

My choice of protein on most days is an egg or two. Filling and easy to prepare, they can be eaten and seasoned in a million different ways.

Hard-Boiled Eggs

I always have a couple of hard-boiled eggs tucked away in the refrigerator. My mom usually peels her hard-boiled eggs under running water to avoid burning her fingers as soon as they come out of the pot. They make an easy snack, like deviled eggs (page 144). You can turn them into an egg salad (page 143), or add them to soup (page 76).

MAKES 6 HARD-BOILED EGGS

6 large eggs

Fill a large bowl with ice and plenty of cool water. Put the eggs in a medium saucepan and add enough water to cover the eggs by 1 in [2.5 cm]. Bring just to a boil over medium-low heat, and immediately remove from the heat. Let sit, covered with a lid, for 5 minutes. Remove the eggs with a slotted spoon and place them in the ice bath to shock them and stop the cooking. Let cool for 5 minutes. Peel the eggs under running water. To store leftover peeled hard-boiled eggs, put damp paper towels in the container with the eggs to wick away the moisture. You can also store the eggs in their shells in an airtight container in the refrigerator for up to 1 week.

Crispy Fried Eggs in Ghee

Changing one ingredient can radically change the flavor of something as simple as a fried egg. You can season it simply with salt and pepper, but I also recommend a pinch of Garam Masala (page 263) or Bacon-Guajillo Salt (page 267).

MAKES 1 FRIED EGG

1 Tbsp Ghee (page 268), plus more as needed
1 large egg
Sea salt and freshly ground black pepper

Heat the ghee in a small cast-iron or stainless-steel skillet over medium-high heat, swirling to coat. Turn the heat to low. Crack the egg into a small bowl, tip it into the skillet, and cook until the egg white sets and the edges become crispy, about 1½ minutes. Transfer the egg to a plate. If you want the white to set on top of the yolk, cover the skillet while you cook the egg. Season with a little salt and pepper and serve immediately.

Rice

Basmati is generally my rice of choice. It's a long-grain variety with an appealing floral aroma. Keep the following pointers in mind when cooking basmati rice: Always buy aged basmati (it is usually indicated on the package) because as the rice matures, the aroma improves. When cooking plain basmati, don't add salt or oil, as both will kill the rice's aroma. (The one exception is when making a pilaf.) You can add a pinch of saffron or turmeric to give the rice a little color and extra flavor, though. Wash the rice in a fine-mesh strainer under cool running water to prevent the rice grains from sticking together as they cook. And finally, presoak the grains to reduce the cooking time.

Plain Rice

Varieties of rice vary in shape, color, starch, and protein content. My cooking is more successful when I tweak my method to the particular variety. The absorption method I share here is a wonderful way to cook long-grain basmati.

MAKES 2 SERVINGS

1 cup [200 g] basmati rice
4 cups [960 ml] water

Pick through the rice for any stones or debris. Put the rice in a fine-mesh strainer and rinse under cool running water until the runoff is no longer cloudy. Transfer to a medium bowl, cover with 2 cups [480 ml] of the water, and soak for 1 to 1½ hours. Drain the water. Put the rice in a medium saucepan or a small Dutch oven with a lid and add the remaining 2 cups [480 ml] water. Bring to a rolling boil over medium-high heat. Turn the heat to low, cover, and cook until most of the water has evaporated, 10 to 12 minutes. Remove from the heat and let sit, covered, for another 5 minutes. Just before serving, fluff the rice with a fork.

Simple Pilaf

While you can eat this highly aromatic pilaf with almost anything, even a side of plain yogurt, it goes really well with the lamb chops on page 178 or the Brussels sprouts on page 105.

MAKES 2 SERVINGS

1 cup [200 g] basmati rice
4 cups [960 ml] water
1 Tbsp Ghee (page 268)
2 green cardamom pods
1 black cardamom pod
1 tsp cumin seeds
3 or 4 whole cloves
1 bay leaf, fresh or dried

Pick through the rice for any stones or debris. Put the rice in a fine-mesh strainer and rinse under cool running water. Transfer to a medium bowl, cover with 2 cups [480 ml] of the water, and soak for 1 to 1½ hours.

Heat the ghee in a medium saucepan or small Dutch oven over medium-high heat. Crack the cardamom pods with a mortar and pestle and add them to the saucepan along with the cumin, cloves, and bay leaf. Sauté the spices until fragrant, 30 to 45 seconds. Drain the soaked rice and add it to the saucepan. Fry the grains until completely coated with the ghee, 1 to 1½ minutes. Add the remaining 2 cups [480 ml] water and bring to a rolling boil. Lower the heat to a gentle simmer, cover the pan, and cook until most of the water has evaporated, 10 to 12 minutes. Fluff the rice with a fork and serve. (You can remove the whole spices at this stage, but I usually prefer to leave them in.) Any leftovers can be stored in an airtight container in the refrigerator for up to 1 week. To reheat, add 2 Tbsp water to every 1 cup [120 g] of cooked rice and reheat in a saucepan over low heat or in the microwave.

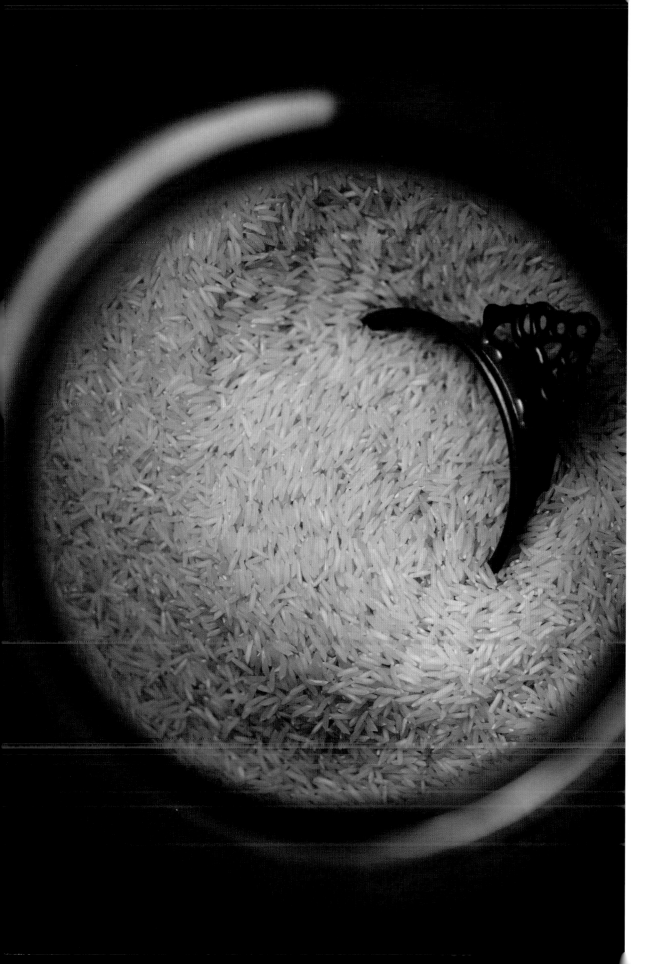

Garlic

Garlic is a powerful seasoning that can be used raw or cooked to mellow its pungency. I usually use less garlic in fresh preparations due to its intense and potent flavor. Remember to sauté minced or sliced garlic just for a few seconds as it burns quickly, and tastes bitter and unpleasant.

Roasted Garlic

Make a batch of these sweet roasted garlic bulbs every other week, and you will find yourself using them to season any and everything. Spread on slices of baguettes, blend into sauces, or add them as a seasoning agent to vinaigrettes and dipping oils like the Roasted Garlic in Sesame Oil (recipe follows).

MAKES 1 ROASTED GARLIC BULB

1 large garlic bulb

2 tsp extra-virgin olive oil

¼ tsp fine sea salt

Preheat the oven to 400°F [200°C]. Peel off and discard most of the outer layer of papery skin on the garlic, and cut off the top quarter of the bulb. Put the garlic on a sheet of aluminum foil large enough to wrap it. Rub or brush with the olive oil and sprinkle with the salt. Wrap in the foil and roast until the cloves feel soft and tender when pricked with a knife, about 1 hour. Remove from the oven, cool for about 45 minutes to 1 hour, and unwrap. To use, squeeze the cloves from their skins. Refrigerate in an airtight container for up to 2 weeks.

Roasted Garlic in Sesame Oil

One of my favorite ways to use roasted garlic is to add a few cloves to sesame oil and sprinkle the oil with salt flakes. You can use this oil as a dip for bread or to flavor fish and meats. It also makes a great seasoning for cold soba noodle salads.

MAKES 1 CUP [185 G]

1 recipe Roasted Garlic (preceding recipe)

1½ tsp flaky sea salt, such as Maldon

½ cup [120 ml] toasted sesame oil, plus more as needed

Put the cooled head of roasted garlic in a clean, dry 8½ oz [250 ml] canning jar with a tight-fitting lid. Sprinkle the salt over the garlic and pour in the sesame oil. Gently stir the garlic to remove any trapped air bubbles and make sure there is enough oil to cover completely. Add more if necessary. Seal the jar and store in the refrigerator for 1 week before using. The flavored oil will keep for up to 1 month in the refrigerator.

Dairy

Dairy is used frequently in Northern Indian cooking. Its soothing and cooling abilities are wonderful, so cheese and yogurt are added to hot and spicy preparations. Here are two of the most frequently stocked items in my refrigerator.

Paneer

One of the easiest cheeses to make, and the only one used in Indian cooking, paneer requires two ingredients: milk and an acid, such as lemon juice. I don't use fat-free milk because the curd doesn't hold up as well when the paneer forms. Unlike regular cheese, paneer doesn't melt; it holds its shape when heated. You can crumble it and use it as a topping in salads, or add chunks to stews, or even roast cubes with vegetables for a salad (see page 64).

MAKES 1 LB 2 OZ [510 G]

---

1 gal [3.8 L] whole milk or reduced-fat milk

¼ cup [60 ml] fresh lemon juice or apple cider vinegar, plus more as needed

Line a large colander with a double layer of cheesecloth, muslin, or another porous white cloth. In a large pot, bring the milk to a rolling boil over medium heat, stirring the milk and scraping the bottom to prevent scalding. Stir in the lemon juice. The milk will curdle and separate (add a little more lemon juice if the milk has not completely curdled). Continue to boil for about 30 seconds, stirring slowly to prevent the large clumps from breaking up. Remove from the heat and pour the whey with the cheese through the lined colander. Hold under cold running water for 15 to 20 seconds to rinse out any traces of the lemon juice. Gather the edges of the cloth, tie them together, and squeeze out as much liquid as you can.

Hang the cloth from the handle of a wooden spoon, and set the spoon over the colander. Allow the water to drain from the cheese for 1 hour at room temperature.

To shape the paneer, place the drained cheese, still in the cloth, on a flat plate. Put a heavy weight, such as a Dutch oven, over the cheese. Let sit for 30 to 45 minutes; any excess water will be extruded and the cheese will be firm to the touch. Remove the paneer from the cloth, and cut and use as needed. Store the paneer, wrapped with plastic wrap in an airtight container, for up to 5 days in the refrigerator.

Kefir Crème Fraîche

Crème fraîche is a luxurious ingredient. It has a velvety smooth texture and a mildly sweet and tangy taste. And because it has a much more interesting flavor profile than heavy cream, I use it often in both sweet and savory dishes.

Buttermilk is often used to ferment the cream, but I prefer using kefir. It contains yeast in addition to lactobacilli, and together they create a silkier and more puddinglike crème fraîche with a richer flavor.

MAKES 1 CUP [200 G]

---

1 Tbsp full-fat kefir

1 cup [240 ml] heavy cream

In a sterile 1 pt [480 ml] canning jar with a tight-fitting lid, combine the kefir and the heavy cream. Stir with a spoon and cover with a clean piece of cheesecloth. Keep in a warm place (preferably 71°F [22°C]) until it thickens, at least 24 hours. Remove the cheesecloth and seal the jar. Store in the refrigerator for 48 hours before using. Keep refrigerated, and use within 2 weeks.

Spice Blends

Here are a couple of spice blends (masalas) that I always keep in my kitchen. It is better to make ground spice blends in small batches and use them within a few months, or they start to lose their potency.

Garam Masala

Most families in the Indian subcontinent have a stash of garam masala in their kitchen; the ratios of the spices differ from region to region. Use this spice mixture as an all-purpose, savory seasoning by letting it bloom a little in hot oil (page 161) at the start of cooking or adding directly later in the cooking process.

MAKES ABOUT ¼ CUP [25 G]

2 Tbsp cumin seeds

2 Tbsp coriander seeds

1 Tbsp black peppercorns

2 dried bay leaves

One 2 in [5 cm] cinnamon stick

12 whole cloves

1 tsp whole black cardamom pods

1 tsp whole green cardamom pods

1 tsp freshly grated nutmeg

½ tsp ground mace

Heat a small, dry stainless-steel or cast-iron skillet over medium-high heat. Turn the heat to medium-low and add the cumin seeds, coriander seeds, peppercorns, bay leaves, cinnamon stick, cloves, and black and green cardamom pods. Toast gently, shaking the pan, until the spices become fragrant, 30 to 45 seconds. Be careful not to burn the spices; if they do burn, discard and start fresh.

Transfer the toasted spices to a mortar or spice grinder. Add the nutmeg and mace and grind to a fine powder. Store the spice mix in an airtight container in a cool, dark place for up to 6 months.

Chaat Masala

This mix can be used with both savory and sweet preparations, but it's especially good in dishes with some acidity, which enhances its flavor. *Kala namak*, a black salt used in Indian cooking, is traditionally included in dishes made with this spice blend. It's available at most Asian and Indian grocery stores in both rock and ground form. Use ¼ tsp powdered *Kala namak* to every 1 tsp of chaat masala.

MAKES ABOUT ¼ CUP [25 G]

2 tsp carom seeds

2 tsp cumin seeds

2 tsp coriander seeds

4 dried Kashmiri chiles

4 whole cloves

1 tsp dried mint

1 tsp ground ginger

1 tsp amchur

Pinch of asafetida

1 tsp black peppercorns

In a small, dry stainless-steel or cast-iron skillet over medium-high heat, toast the carom, cumin, and coriander seeds until fragrant, swirling the spices occasionally so they toast evenly, 30 to 45 seconds.

Transfer the toasted spices to a mortar or a spice grinder and add the remaining ingredients. Grind to a fine powder. Store the spice mix in an airtight container in a cool, dark place for up to 1 month.

My Za'atar Blend

Za'atar is a Middle Eastern seasoning I turn to often to finish off a bowl of freshly ground hummus, season roasted vegetables or grilled skewers of meat, or add to hot ghee then drizzle over a bowl of steaming rice

MAKES ABOUT ¼ CUP [50 G]

2 Tbsp white sesame seeds

1 Tbsp dried oregano

1 Tbsp dried thyme

1 Tbsp ground sumac

1 Tbsp ground cumin

1 Tbsp red chili flakes

1 tsp freshly ground black pepper

Combine all the ingredients in a small bowl. Stir together and transfer to an airtight container. Store, covered, in a cool, dark place for up to 4 months.

Chai Masala

Chai is the Hindi word for "tea," and in most Indian households, cups of hot chai are served with snacks and sweets every evening when people come back from work. Indians drink chai in many different and beautiful ways, from simply steeping the tea leaves in hot water to accompanying the leaves with a masala (spice blend). Some add dried herbs, such as mint or holy basil (*tulsi*), or a few strands of saffron. My mom usually adds 1 tsp of freshly grated ginger to every cup of tea she brews, and occasionally a cracked pod of green cardamom.

MAKES ¼ CUP [25 G]

Seeds from 10 green cardamom pods, crushed

Seeds from 1 whole black cardamom pod

6 black peppercorns

4 whole cloves

One 1 in [2.5 cm] piece cinnamon stick

1 Tbsp ground ginger

Grind the cardamom seeds, peppercorns, cloves, and cinnamon stick with a mortar and pestle or a spice grinder. Transfer to an airtight container, stir in the ginger, and cover. Store the masala in a cool, dark place for up to 1 month.

Masala Chai

When masala (spice blend) is brewed with tea, it is called Masala Chai. This is my basic recipe for how to prepare masala chai. After preparing the tea, add as much milk or sweetener as you like. (I prefer the taste of maple syrup or brown sugar.) Although milk is traditional, you can also leave it out. In India, folks like to cool their tea by pouring it back and forth between glasses until it is cool enough to sip.

MAKES 2 SERVINGS

2 cups [480 ml] water

1 tsp Chai Masala (preceding recipe)

2 tsp black tea leaves, such as Darjeeling or Assam

¼ cup [60 ml] hot milk

Maple syrup or brown sugar for serving (optional)

In a medium saucepan over medium-high heat, bring the water and masala to a rolling boil. Turn the heat to low and add the tea leaves. Return the water to a boil and let it boil for 1 full minute. Remove from the heat and let it sit and steep for 1 to 2 minutes longer, depending on how strong you want your brew. Stir in the milk, taste, and add maple syrup or brown sugar, if desired. Strain through a small fine-mesh strainer set over a teapot, and serve hot.

Salt Blends

Seasoning with flavored salts is one of the easiest ways to add finesse to your cooking. By taking your inspiration from the spices, herbs, and other aromatics in your pantry, you can create an array of salts in different flavors and colors. Use them to season your vegetables, soups, and broths, and as a garnish for the rims of your cocktail glasses.

Curry and Makrut Lime Leaf Salt

Use this wonderful salt to rim a cocktail glass. It adds the fresh and unmistakable aromas of curry and lime to snacks such as roasted nuts or a salad. This can be made with curry or makrut lime leaves.

MAKES ¼ CUP [70 G]

12 fresh curry leaves

6 fresh makrut lime leaves

¼ cup [65 g] fine sea salt

Rinse the curry and makrut lime leaves under cool running water and dab them dry with paper towels. Tear the leaves into pieces and put them in a spice grinder, along with the salt. Pulse until you get a fine powder. Transfer to an airtight container, cover, and store at room temperature for up to 2 weeks.

Bacon-Guajillo Salt

We keep a small jar of this on our dining table at all times to add a little bit of smokiness and heat to savory dishes.

MAKES ½ CUP [70 G]

3 strips bacon

1 Tbsp ground guajillo chile

½ cup [60 g] flaky sea salt, such as Maldon

Preheat the oven to 400°F [200°C]. Put a wire rack on a baking sheet and lay the bacon strips on the rack. Cook in the oven for 15 to 20 minutes, until crispy, flipping the strips over halfway through cooking. Remove the bacon with tongs and drain on paper towels. (Discard the fat in the baking sheet or store in the refrigerator for another use.) When the bacon is cool enough to handle, chop it into tiny bits.

In a small bowl, mix the bacon, guajillo chile, and salt together. Transfer to an airtight container, cover, and store for up to 1 month in a cool dark place at room temperature.

Nori and Yuzu Ponzu Salt

Sprinkle on freshly shucked oysters—or any seafood for that matter.

MAKES ¼ CUP [40 G]

¼ cup [60 ml] *yuzu ponzu* sauce

¼ cup [30 g] flaky sea salt, such as Maldon

1 Tbsp white sesame seeds

1½ tsp chopped nori

Preheat the oven to 200°F [95°C]. In a small bowl, mix together the *yuzu ponzu*, salt, sesame seeds, and nori. Spread out on a ceramic or nonreactive baking sheet. Cover with plastic wrap and refrigerate for 20 minutes. Unwrap the baking sheet and cook the salt blend until all the liquid in the pan has evaporated, 4 to 6 hours. With a silicone spatula, scrape the blend into a resealable plastic bag or a jar with a lid. Put the bag or jar inside another resealable plastic bag, this time with a little raw rice in it. The seasoning mix tends to be hygroscopic, meaning it absorbs moisture quickly, and this arrangement will help keep it dry. Store at room temperature for up to 2 weeks.

Fats

Not only are there a wide variety of fats to choose from, but they are also excellent vehicles to carry flavor. Just heat them up before adding spices to infuse them.

Ghee

Ghee is one of the most popular fats used in Indian cooking. It is a form of clarified butter, from which the milk solids and water are removed. Because the milk solids and sugars are caramelized in the fat before their removal, they give the ghee a nutty fragrance. Ghee can last for months if stored correctly, because the water, sugar, and proteins are all removed.

MAKES APPROXIMATELY 1¼ CUPS [250 G]

---

1 lb [455 g] unsalted butter, cubed

Line a strainer with a few layers of cheesecloth and place over a clean, dry 1 pt [480 ml] jar with a tight-fitting lid to hold the finished ghee. Set aside.

In a heavy, medium saucepan over medium-high heat, melt the butter, stirring occasionally with a large metal spoon. As the butter starts to melt, skim off and discard any foam that rises to the surface. Cook until all the water in the butter boils off, and the fat stops sizzling and turns a deep golden yellow. The milk solids at the bottom of the saucepan will be reddish brown. The entire process should take 12 to 15 minutes. Remove the saucepan from the heat and carefully pour the liquid through the cheesecloth-lined strainer into the jar. Seal the jar and store the ghee in a cool, dark place for up to 3 months, or indefinitely in the refrigerator.

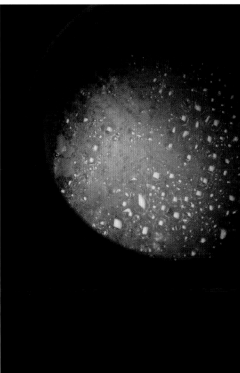

My Nit'r Qibe

Nit'r qibe is a very tasty fat that forms the basis of many Ethiopian recipes. It's quite similar to ghee, but it contains milk solids, and it is seasoned with spices. You can cook with it as you would ghee or any other fat. I've been known to dip pieces of bread into a warmed jar of *nit'r qibe*, to which I've added a little salt.

MAKES 2 CUPS [120 G]

1 cup [220 g] unsalted butter, cubed

¼ cup [35 g] finely chopped red onion

1 tsp finely chopped garlic

One 1 in [2.5 cm] piece fresh ginger, peeled and grated

1 black cardamom pod, crushed

1 tsp cumin seeds

1 tsp fenugreek seeds

1 tsp nigella seeds

1 tsp dried oregano

1 tsp ground turmeric

Line a fine-mesh strainer with a few layers of cheese-cloth and place over a clean, dry 1 pt [480 ml] jar with a tight-fitting lid to hold the finished *nit'r qibe*.

In a medium saucepan over medium-low heat, melt the butter. Add the onion, garlic, and ginger and cook, skimming off and discarding any foam that rises to the surface, until the butter is completely clear, about 30 minutes. Carefully pour through the cheesecloth-lined strainer into the jar. Stir the cracked cardamom pod, cumin seeds, fenugreek seeds, nigella seeds, oregano, and turmeric into the hot fat and seal. Store the *nit'r qibe* in the refrigerator for up to 3 months.

Spiced Sweet Honey Butter

I keep a batch of this compound butter in my refrigerator at all times. The fat in the butter takes on the colors of the ground toasted spices, resulting in a deep golden butter that's fragrant, salty, and sweet.

You can use this butter any way you like. I slather it on good sourdough, warm toast, or flatbread. I even spoon it onto baked salmon or mackerel and then finish with a drizzle of lemon juice.

MAKES 1 CUP [230 G]

½ tsp red chili flakes

½ tsp fennel seeds

½ tsp black sesame seeds

½ tsp white sesame seeds

½ tsp poppy seeds

½ tsp coriander seeds

¼ tsp ground cardamom

3 black peppercorns

1 cup [230 g] European-style unsalted butter, cubed, at room temperature

1 Tbsp honey

2 tsp flaky sea salt, such as Maldon

Heat a small, dry stainless-steel or cast-iron skillet over medium-high heat. Add the chili flakes and all the spices and seeds, including the peppercorns. Toast until fragrant and the fennel and coriander seeds start to brown, swirling the spices occasionally so they toast evenly, 30 to 45 seconds. Grind the hot spice mixture with a mortar and pestle or a spice grinder to a coarse powder. Transfer to a medium bowl and add the butter, honey, and salt, mashing with a fork to combine. Shape the compound butter into a log and wrap with parchment paper. Refrigerate for at least 2 hours to firm up before serving. Store in an airtight container in the refrigerator for up to 3 weeks.

Pickles

These quick pickles can be made in as little as a few hours and require little more effort than a few shakes of a lidded jar.

Pickled Green Tomatoes with Mixed Peppercorns

This recipe was borne out of necessity, from an end-of-season abundance of green tomatoes. I use these to top grilled burgers and kebab sandwiches.

MAKES 1 CUP [220 G]

1 Tbsp rainbow peppercorns

½ cup [120 ml] rice wine vinegar

¼ cup [60 ml] mirin

½ tsp fine sea salt

½ tsp sugar

¼ tsp long pepper

1 cup [130 g] small green tomatoes

With a mortar and pestle, lightly crack the peppercorns. Transfer to a small, nonreactive saucepan and add the vinegar, mirin, salt, sugar, and long pepper. Bring to a boil over medium-high heat. Remove from the heat and cool completely. Fish out the peppercorns, leaving the liquid in the saucepan, and set aside.

Remove the stems from the tomatoes and, using a sharp paring knife, cut the tomatoes crosswise into thin rounds.

Put a third of the reserved peppercorns in the bottom of a clean 1 pt [480 ml] canning jar with a tight-fitting lid. Arrange a third of the tomatoes on top. Repeat the layers twice more. Pour enough of the remaining liquid in the saucepan over the tomatoes to cover. Seal the jar and refrigerate for at least 3 days, shaking the jar gently once every day. The pickled tomatoes will keep in the refrigerator for up to 1 week.

Pickled Carrot with Fennel

I squeeze this quick carrot pickle into my sandwiches to add an extra burst of flavor in each bite.

MAKES 1 CUP [200 G]

1 cup [70 g] thinly sliced carrot

1 tsp fennel seeds

½ cup [120 ml] fresh lime juice

1 tsp honey or maple syrup

½ tsp fine sea salt

Put the carrots in a clean 1 pt [480 ml] canning jar with a tight-fitting lid.

In a small, dry skillet over medium-high heat, toast the fennel seeds until fragrant, 30 to 45 seconds, swirling the seeds occasionally so they toast evenly. Quickly transfer to the jar.

In a small bowl, whisk together the lime juice, honey, and salt. Pour over the carrots and fennel seeds. Seal the jar and shake a few times. Refrigerate for at least 2 hours before serving. Store in the refrigerator for up to 3 days.

Red Onions with Coriander

This is my go-to pickle when I make kebabs, providing contrast in hot, spicy dishes.

MAKES 1 CUP [220 G]

1 cup [100 g] thinly sliced red onion

1 Tbsp fresh cilantro leaves

1 tsp coriander seeds

½ cup [120 ml] apple cider vinegar

¼ tsp sugar

⅛ tsp fine sea salt

Put the onions and cilantro in a clean 1 pt [480 ml] canning jar with a tight-fitting lid.

In a small, dry cast-iron or stainless-steel skillet, toast the coriander seeds over medium-high heat, until fragrant, swirling the seeds occasionally so they toast evenly, 30 to 45 seconds. Toss the seeds into the jar with the onions. Add the vinegar, sugar, and salt. Seal the jar and shake a few times. Refrigerate for at least 2 hours before serving. Store in the refrigerator for up to 3 days.

Ginger-Lemon Relish

In India, my dad makes this relish often to eat at lunch or dinner. I add the ginger slices to fresh salads.

MAKES 1 CUP [245 G]

One 2 in [5 cm] piece fresh ginger, peeled and thinly sliced

½ cup [120 ml] fresh lemon juice

¼ tsp fine sea salt

Put the ginger slices in the bottom of a clean 1 pt [480 ml] canning jar with a tight-fitting lid. Add the lemon juice and salt. Seal the jar and shake a few times. Refrigerate for 2 hours before serving. Store the relish in the refrigerator for up to 2 days.

Spiced Lemon Pickle

In India, pickles are often prepared by preserving vegetables or fruit in mustard oil. Because mustard oil is not sold in America, I've created a recipe made with olive oil. The leftover oil is very versatile; it's wonderful for dipping bread or naan or drizzling over hot pizza (page 99), baked fish, or even roasted vegetables.

MAKES 4½ LB [2 KG]

2 lb [910 g] lemons, quartered and seeded

¼ cup [60 ml] fresh lemon juice

⅔ cup [200 g] fine sea salt

2 Tbsp plus 1 tsp [15 g] black peppercorns

¼ cup [15 g] red chili flakes

1 Tbsp plus 2 tsp [15 g] fenugreek seeds

1 Tbsp [7 g] cumin seeds

4½ cups [1 L] extra-virgin olive oil

Combine the lemons, lemon juice, and salt in a clean 3 qt [2.8 L] canning jar with a tight-fitting lid. Seal and shake to combine. Let sit for 30 minutes.

Combine the peppercorns, red chili flakes, fenugreek seeds, and cumin seeds in a mortar and crush lightly with a pestle to crack the spices. Transfer the spice mix to the jar, and add the olive oil. Seal and shake a few times. Put the jar in a cool, dark place and shake once a day for 1 week before serving. Store in a cool, dark place at room temperature for up to 1 month. Or store the pickle in the refrigerator for up to 2 months. Let the cold pickle sit at room temperature for about 30 minutes to warm before using.

Condiments and Sauces

I rely on a variety of condiments to add a bright spot of flavor to my meals. Some can go on the side and compliment other dishes; others can be folded into salads or used as seasoning. Here is a collection of some of my go-to (lifesaving!) pantry essentials.

Charred Green Garlic and Yuzu Ponzu Sauce

This is a good sauce to drizzle over grilled vegetables or meat, or even hard-boiled eggs. And it is also great in a salad made with cold soba noodles.

MAKES 1 CUP [240 G]

3 green garlic stalks

1 Tbsp vegetable oil

2 green Thai chiles

¼ cup [60 ml] *yuzu ponzu* sauce

¼ cup [60 ml] verjus blanc (white verjus)

1 tsp fine sea salt

¼ cup [60 ml] toasted sesame oil

Preheat the grill to high and brush the grates with a little oil. Rinse the green garlic under cold running water and trim off any damaged or dried ends on the green stalks. Pat dry with paper towels and brush the stalks with the vegetable oil. Place the garlic stalks on the hot grill for 4 to 5 minutes, flipping them over when they acquire deep grill marks and a nice char. The roots will turn ashy and burn. Transfer the green garlic, including the burned bits, to a blender and add the chiles, *yuzu ponzu* sauce, and verjus. Pulse until you get a coarse sauce, just a few seconds. Transfer to a clean canning jar with a tight-fitting lid and stir in the salt and sesame oil. Seal the jar and store in the refrigerator for up to 2 weeks.

Hot Green Chutney

What started out as an idea to use leftover greens in the refrigerator quickly became one of the most versatile condiments in my kitchen. Fresh baby kale and peppery arugula leaves are transformed into a vibrant green chutney, with a few serrano chiles for a blast of heat. If you want your chutney even hotter, substitute fresh Thai chiles. I make this with baby kale, which is a little sweeter than regular kale. Use it as a dipping sauce for the Chickpea-Battered Fried Okra (page 38) or marinate a whole chicken in it before roasting (page 147).

MAKES 2 CUPS [470 G]

2 cups [120 g] arugula leaves

1 cup [60 g] packed baby kale leaves

¼ cup [60 ml] extra-virgin olive oil, preferably Arbequina

¼ cup [60 ml] water

½ cup [70 g] chopped red onion

2 Tbsp fresh lime juice

4 garlic cloves

4 serrano chiles

1 tsp caraway seeds

1 tsp coriander seeds

1 tsp cumin seeds

1 tsp fine sea salt

Combine all the ingredients in a blender and pulse on medium-low speed for 1 to 2 minutes, until you get a coarse paste. You might need to stop the blender to move things around. Taste and adjust the seasoning, if necessary. Transfer the sauce to an airtight container and store for up to 2 weeks in the refrigerator or up to 1 month in the freezer.

Sweet and Smoky Tahini Sauce

Try this creamy sauce with crab cakes (page 123). It's also great with fish and vegetables.

MAKES 2 CUPS [510 G]

1 cup [220 g] tahini

1 cup [240 ml] hot water

¼ cup [60 ml] fresh lemon juice

2 Tbsp pomegranate molasses

2 Tbsp ground chipotle chile, plus more for garnish

½ tsp fine sea salt

Combine all the ingredients in a blender and pulse on medium-high speed until smooth and creamy. Let stand for 10 minutes before serving. Store in an airtight container in the refrigerator for up to 2 weeks.

Cilantro Oil Dressing

Try this fresh herb dressing as a dipping sauce or toss it with roasted cauliflower in a salad (page 64). It's also great over grilled steaks and seafood.

MAKES 1 CUP [240 G]

1 cup [240 ml] extra-virgin olive oil

1 cup [20 g] tightly packed fresh cilantro leaves

1 serrano chile, seeded, if desired

Juice of 1 lime

1 tsp coriander seeds

½ tsp black peppercorns

½ tsp fine sea salt

Combine all the ingredients in a blender and pulse at medium-high speed until smooth and pastelike. Store in an airtight container in the refrigerator for up to 4 days. Shake before using.

Spicy Rhubarb Confit

Though most people associate rhubarb with dessert, I've made it my mission in life to use it in savory dishes whenever possible. This confit pairs the acidity of rhubarb with hot Thai chiles and makrut lime leaves. The result is a great dipping sauce or an all-purpose condiment. The type of olive oil you use will affect the flavor of this confit.

MAKES 4 CUPS [920 G]

10 oz [280 g] pearl onions

1 lb [455 g] rhubarb stalks, ends trimmed

1¾ oz [50 g] mixed red and green Thai chiles, halved lengthwise, and seeded if desired

6 fresh makrut lime leaves or lemon leaves

1 tsp fine sea salt

2 cups [480 ml] extra-virgin olive oil

Preheat the oven to 250°F [110°C].

While the oven is heating, fill a medium saucepan with water and bring to a rolling boil. Fill a medium bowl with ice water. Using a paring knife, trim both ends of the pearl onions and plunge the onions into the boiling water for 30 seconds. Using a slotted spoon, transfer to the ice water to stop the cooking. Drain and put the onions on a clean kitchen towel or paper towels and dab dry. Using the paring knife, remove the skins and halve the onions lengthwise.

Cut the rhubarb crosswise into 1 in [2.5 cm] pieces.

In a medium bowl, combine the rhubarb, onions, chiles, makrut lime leaves, and salt. Add the olive oil and toss to combine. Transfer to a shallow baking dish and bake until the rhubarb chunks are tender and almost mushy, about 3 hours. Remove the dish from the oven and cool completely. Transfer the confit to an airtight container and refrigerate for up to 1 month.

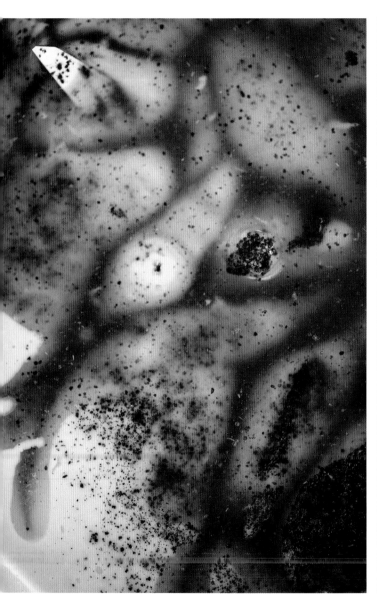

Apple and Pear Mostarda

Italian mostardas are like spiced preserves. They live at the intersection between sweet and sour and are traditionally prepared by cooking fruit with mustard seeds. In this apple and pear version, I add dried juniper berries and a dash of verjus blanc to the mustard and fruit.

MAKES 2 CUPS [510 G]

1 large Bartlett pear (8½ oz [240 g])

2 large Honeycrisp apples (8 oz [225 g] each)

3 Tbsp Dijon mustard

2 Tbsp sugar

2 Tbsp yellow mustard seeds

1 Tbsp dried juniper berries

2 Tbsp water

1 Tbsp food-grade mustard oil or
   extra-virgin olive oil

¼ cup [60 ml] verjus blanc (white verjus)

Peel and core the pear and apples, and cut them into ¼ in [6 mm] dice. Combine the fruit with the remaining ingredients in a medium nonreactive saucepan, such as stainless steel. Cook over medium-high heat, stirring occasionally, until the fruit is soft and most of the liquid has evaporated, 25 to 30 minutes. Transfer to an airtight container and store in the refrigerator for up to 1 month.

Blackberry Long Pepper Jam

Long pepper is a little more fiery than the more common black peppercorn and is frequently used to prepare savory Indian pickles.

MAKES 2½ CUPS [605 G]

1 tsp long pepper

5½ cups [660 g] fresh blackberries

1 cup [200 g] sugar

¼ cup [60 ml] fresh lemon juice

With a mortar and pestle or spice grinder, crush the long pepper to a coarse powder. In a large nonreactive saucepan, such as stainless steel, combine the berries, crushed pepper, sugar, and lemon juice. Bring to a boil over medium-high heat, turn the heat to medium-low, and crush the berries with a potato masher. Cook, stirring occasionally with a silicone spatula, until the jam is thick enough to coat the back of a spoon, about 20 minutes. Transfer to a clean and sterile 1 pt [480 ml] canning jar with a tight-fitting lid and seal the jar. Store in the refrigerator for up to 1 week.

Green Mango Tartar Sauce

Unripe green mango brightens this sauce, perfect with seafood.

MAKES 1 CUP [240 G]

1 cup [240 g] mayonnaise

2 Tbsp finely chopped green (unripe) mango

1 Tbsp minced shallots

2 Tbsp fresh lemon juice

Sea salt and ground white pepper

In a medium bowl, gently mix together the mayonnaise, mango, shallots, and lemon juice. Season with the salt and white pepper.

RESOURCES

Here are some of my favorite places to buy spices in the United States.

East Coast

KALUSTYAN'S

123 Lexington Avenue
New York, NY 10016
www.kalustyans.com

LA BOÎTE

724 Eleventh Avenue
New York, NY 10019
www.laboiteny.com

PENZEYS SPICES

1293 Massachusetts Avenue
Arlington, MA 02474
www.penzeys.com

BAZAAR SPICES

1309 Fifth Street NE
Washington, DC 20002
www.bazaarspices.com

Midwest

THE SPICE HOUSE

1512 North Wells Street
Chicago, IL 60610
www.thespicehouse.com

PENZEYS SPICES

3208 Hennepin Avenue S
Minneapolis, MN 55408
www.penzeys.com

South

BUFORD HIGHWAY FARMERS' MARKET

5600 Buford Highway NE
Atlanta, GA 30340
www.aofwc.com

West Coast

OAKTOWN SPICE SHOP

546 Grand Avenue
Oakland, CA 94610
www.oaktownspiceshop.com

SPICE ACE

1821 Steiner Street
San Francisco, CA 94115
www.spiceace.com

SPICE STATION

3819 W. Sunset Boulevard
Los Angeles, CA 90026
www.spicestationsilverlake.com

MARKET SPICE

85A Pike Place
Seattle, WA 98101
www.marketspice.com

ACKNOWLEDGMENTS

A cookbook is the sum of many moving parts. It took me two years to complete this book, but the actual journey began much earlier, and my path was paved by the kindness of several people.

THANK YOU TO:

My readers of both *A Brown Table* and A Brown Kitchen. You've been with me from the start when I grabbed my Nikon COOLPIX to document my food through my blog, *A Brown Table*, from my tiny kitchen in Washington, D.C. You've lifted and carried me all the way on this long road with your love and encouragement. This book is as much yours as it is mine and none of this would be possible without you.

My fearless agent, Maria Ribas at Stonesong Literary, who has been my knight in shining armor and guided me through the daunting process of navigating a book deal and, above all, has believed in me and my work.

My patient and tireless editor, Sarah Billingsley, who worked feverishly to help me shape and craft this book and share my story. The phenomenally talented Alice Chau for bringing my vision to life with her stunning designs, letting me be a part of the process, putting up with my crazy ideas, and teaching me that font choices are a reflection of your personality. I also want to give a special shout-out to Alexandra Brown, Amy Treadwell, Tera Killip, Marie Oishi, Steve Kim, and the rest of the incredible team at Chronicle Books who worked behind the scenes to bring this book to fruition.

John Birdsall, for your generous words and mentorship but, above all, your friendship. You and Perry have both become wonderful neighbors and close friends ever since we moved to Oakland.

Asha Gomez, Meera Sodha, Cyrus Todiwala, Nigella Lawson, Diana Henry, Madhur Jaffrey, Niloufer Ichaporia King, Julie Sahni, Matt Rodbard, Daniella Galarza, Alice Medrich, Kat Kinsman, Tundey Wey, Tejal Rao, Joe Yonan, Julia Turshen, Khushbu Shah, Kathy Gunst, Carolyn Phillips, Bryant Terry, Naomi Duguid, Samin Nosrat, Mayukh Sen, Raghavan Iyer, David Lebovitz, Tara O'Brady, and Sonia Chopra: You inspire me in more ways than you can ever imagine through your incredible food and words that continue to change the world.

My editor, Paolo Lucchesi, and the entire team at the Food and Home section at the *San Francisco Chronicle*, I've learned so much from you. Thank you, Paolo, for taking a chance and giving me the opportunity to write A Brown Kitchen. Jonathan Kauffman and Sarah Fritsche, thank you for being my trusty cake taste testers.

Cheryl Sternman Rule, for meticulously sifting through my manuscript and being my second set of eyes.

My friends: Lukas Volger, Steve Viksjo, Ben Mims, Andy Barghani, Chitra Agrawal, Phi Tran, Tina Antolini, Tyler Kalogeros Treschuk, Susan and Terrance Treschuk, Javier de Diego, Samantha Scheidler, Eduardo Sardiña, Justin Bras, Farouk Ophaso, Jessica Nolan, Meghana Hemphill, and Urmila Kamath. All of you have been a part of this book in one way or another. I'm indebted to you for your love and unwavering support, and I'm extremely fortunate to have all of you in my life.

Erica Perez and John Beaver of Oaktown Spice Shop for sharing your treasure trove of knowledge on the world of spices.

My recipe testers, thank you for graciously testing my recipes: Emma Rudolph, Mick Côté, John Wilburn, Matt Walker, Alex Orr, Jeff Reed, Nalini Mani, Nastassia Abad, Sarah Kieffer, Alicia Boal, Peter Holm, Dana Dantzler, Katerina Rangelova, David Hicks, Brittney Timmins, Jennifer Baron, Philip Krupansky, Dana Juhász Ardell, Karen Ho, Jennifer Oberoi, Suzanne Romaine, Francisco Lobo, Ung Soh Fong, Samantha Moullet, Elysse Voyer, Kala Patel, Jenna Homen, Melissa Morton, Tracie Burgess, LaRae Burk, Harsha Mallajosyula, Kris Osborne, Jeremy Aldridge, Huxley McCorkle, Amadon Coletsis, Alicia Prodromou, Benjamin-Edouard Savoie, Paula Casimiro, Annika Patel, Deborah Kravitz, Michelle Rolfe, Laurie Mueller, Eva Wang, Chandrima Sarkar, Diann Leo, Kathleen Hayes, Rochelle Ramos, Barbara Slegers-Hudson, Madrid Jaramillo-Cattell, Kathy Jollimore, Vera Trifonova, Jaime Woo, Sean Conway, Leah Langdon Henry, Tacia Coleman, Scott Peabody, Sophie Mackenzie, Amrita Singh, Suchi Modi, David Hicks, Harriet Trezevant, and Cheryl Gomes.

Williams Sonoma, West Elm, StaubUSA, and Miyabi USA for providing many of the elegant ceramics, linens, and cookware that I used to style the food photographed in this book. The folks of Vitamix, KitchenAid, and California Olive Ranch for their spectacular kitchen tools and ingredients.

My family. My parents, Lorraine and Neelkant, who let me mess up their kitchen, when I first started learning how to cook, and steal their cookbooks. They never complained. My sister, Nishtha, who sent some of the gorgeous props that she painstakingly hunted down in India. My grandmother, Lucy, and aunts Elaine, Valerie, and Bernie, who've taught me to cook over the years. Joy Furtado for opening up her home and kitchen in Goa and sharing her wealth of knowledge on cooking Goan food. My in-laws, especially my mother-in-law, Shelly, for graciously sharing her kitchen at her farm and pushing me to start a blog all those years ago.

Last but not least, my husband, Michael, and our two fur babies, Snoopy and Vesper, who make me laugh and smile even when I'm tired, frantically trying to make deadlines, and who keep me grounded. I love you.

A

Aleppo pepper, 23
Almonds
    Fennel and Ginger–Spiced Sweet Granola,
      91–93
    Roast Leg of Lamb, 181–83
    Saffron and Cardamom Milk, 235
Amchur, 25
Anardana, 25, 37
Apples
    Apple and Pear Mostarda, 281
    Apple and Serrano Slaw, 186–87
    Apple Masala Chai Cake, 207–9
Apricots
    Rum-Soaked Raisin Caramel Cake, 220–21
Artichoke Hearts, Baked Eggs with, 140
Arugula
    Hot Green Chutney, 277
Asafetida, 29

B

Bacon–Guajillo Salt, 267
Basil Yogurt Sauce, 40
Bay leaves, 29
Beans
    Cocoa-Spiced Bean and Lentil Soup, 73
    Smoked Sardines and Kumquat Crostini, 47
Bebinca, Sweet Potato, 204–6
Beef
    Beef Stew with Verjus, 170–71
    Bone and Lentil Broth, 80–81
    Spiced Beef Kebabs, 52
    Spiced Meat Loaf, 167–69
    Steak with Orange Peel and Coriander, 173
Beets
    Rainbow Root Raita, 63
Bellini with Cardamom and Peppercorns, 240
Blackberry Long Pepper Jam, 281
Black peppercorn, 23
Bombay Frittata, 137
Bone and Lentil Broth, 80–81
Bourbon Iced Chai, Caramelized Fig and, 247
Brandy
    Bellini with Cardamom and Peppercorns,
      240
Bread. *See also* Naan
    Baked Eggs with Artichoke Hearts, 140
    Smoked Sardines and Kumquat Crostini, 47
Brining, 161
Broths
    Bone and Lentil Broth, 80–81
    Turmeric and Lime Mussel Broth, 116

Browning, 163
Brown sugar, 25
Bruising, 158
Brussels Sprouts, Shaved, with Poppy Seeds,
    Black Mustard, and Coconut Oil, 105
Butter
    Ghee, 268
    My Nit'r Qibe, 270
    Spiced Sweet Honey Butter, 270
Butternut Squash and Tea Soup, 70

C

Cakes
    Apple Masala Chai Cake, 207–9
    Date and Tamarind Loaf, 210–11
    Elderflower and Ghee Cake, 215
    Rum-Soaked Raisin Caramel Cake, 220–21
    Upside-Down Orange and Fennel Cornmeal
      Cake, 216–18
Cantaloupe Salsa, Corn and, 130
Caprese Salad with Sweet Tamarind Dressing,
    60
Caraway seed, 27
Cardamom, 27
    Bellini with Cardamom and Peppercorns,
      240
    Cardamom Iced Coffee with Coconut Milk,
      239
    Rhubarb, Cardamom, and Rose Water
      Sharbat, 231
    Saffron and Cardamom Milk, 235
Carom seed, 27
Carrots
    Pickled Carrot with Fennel, 273
    Rainbow Root Raita, 63
    Roasted Young Carrots with Sesame, Chili,
      and Nori, 109
Cashews
    Chile-Sumac-Pomegranate Nuts, 37
    Crème Fraîche Chicken Salad, 148–49
    Fennel and Ginger–Spiced Sweet Granola,
      91–93
    Rum-Soaked Raisin Caramel Cake, 220–21
    Savory Granola, 93
    Spiced Mango Milkshake, 236
Cauliflower, Paneer, and Mixed Lentil Salad,
    Roasted, 64
Cayenne pepper, 23
Chaat Masala, 263
    Chaat Masala–Grilled Pork Chops, 184–85
Chai, 264
    Apple Masala Chai Cake, 207–9
    Caramelized Fig and Bourbon Iced Chai, 247

Chai Masala, 264
    Masala Chai, 264
Champagne
    Bellini with Cardamom and Peppercorns,
      240
Cheese. *See also* Paneer
    Baked Eggs with Artichoke Hearts, 140
    Caprese Salad with Sweet Tamarind
      Dressing, 60
    Margherita Naan Pizza, 99
Cherry-Fennel Barbecue Sauce, 152
Chicken
    Chicken Noodle Soup with Omani Limes, 79
    Crème Fraîche Chicken Salad, 148–49
    Curry Leaf Popcorn Chicken, 48–49
    Hot Green Chutney–Roasted Chicken, 147
    shopping for, 136
    Toasted Naan and Chicken Soup, 76–77
Chickpea-Battered Fried Okra, 38
Chiles, 86
    Bacon-Guajillo Salt, 267
    Chile-Sumac-Pomegranate Nuts, 37
    Chipotle–Garam Masala Olives, 34
    storing, 82
    Turmeric-and-Chile-Roasted Red Snapper
      with Melon Salsa, 130–31
    varieties of, 23
Chocolate
    cocoa powder, 29
    Cocoa-Spiced Bean and Lentil Soup, 73
    Spicy Chocolate Chip–Hazelnut Cookies, 203
Chopping, 158
Chouriço
    Chouriço Potato Salad, 69
    Homemade Goan-Style Chouriço, 191
Chutney, Hot Green, 277
Cilantro, 29
    Cilantro Oil Dressing, 278
Cinnamon, 23
Cocoa powder, 29
    Cocoa-Spiced Bean and Lentil Soup, 73
Coconut milk
    Cardamom Iced Coffee with Coconut Milk,
      239
    Sweet Potato Bebinca, 204–6
    Turmeric and Lime Mussel Broth, 116
    Watermelon-Elderflower Granita, 195
Coconut vinegar, 25
Coffee, 29
    Cardamom Iced Coffee with Coconut Milk,
      239
Color, adding, 86
Cookies, Spicy Chocolate Chip–Hazelnut, 203

Coriander, 27
    Coriander Gravlax, 133
    Red Onions with Coriander, 274
Corn
    Corn and Cantaloupe Salsa, 130
    Toasted Naan and Chicken Soup, 76–77
    Cornmeal Cake, Upside-Down Orange and
      Fennel, 216–18
Crab
    Crab Cakes with Lemongrass and Green
      Mango, 123
    Ginger-Garlic Stir-Fried Crab, 124–26
Cranberries
    Fennel and Ginger–Spiced Sweet Granola,
      91–93
Crème fraîche
    Crème Fraîche Chicken Salad, 148–49
    Kefir Crème Fraîche, 260
    Vanilla Bean Crème Fraîche, 200
Crostini, Smoked Sardines and Kumquat, 47
Cucumber Salad, Toasted Cumin and Lime, 59
Cumin, 27
    Toasted Cumin and Lime Cucumber Salad,
      59
    Toasted Cumin Lemonade, 227
Curry leaves, 20
    Curry and Makrut Lime Leaf Salt, 267
    Curry Leaf Popcorn Chicken, 48–49

D

Dates
    Date and Tamarind Loaf, 210–11
    Grilled Dates and Raisins with Black Pepper
      and Honey, 33
Desserts
    Apple Masala Chai Cake, 207–9
    Date and Tamarind Loaf, 210–11
    Elderflower and Ghee Cake, 215
    Jaggery Ice Cream, 199
    Raspberry-Shiso Sorbet, 196
    Rum-Soaked Raisin Caramel Cake, 220–21
    Spiced Maple–Broiled Peaches, 200–201
    Spicy Chocolate Chip–Hazelnut Cookies, 203
    Sweet Potato Bebinca, 204–6
    Upside-Down Orange and Fennel Cornmeal
      Cake, 216–18
    Watermelon-Elderflower Granita, 195
Deviled Eggs with Creamy Tahini and Za'atar,
    144
Dressings
    Cilantro Oil Dressing, 278
    Tamarind Dressing, 60
Drinks
    Bellini with Cardamom and Peppercorns,
      240
    Caramelized Fig and Bourbon Iced Chai, 247
    Cardamom Iced Coffee with Coconut Milk,
      239

    Ginger and Tamarind Refresher, 228
    Orange Blossom Lemonade, 225
    Pineapple Serrano Gin, 243
    Pomegranate Moscow Mule, 244
    Rhubarb, Cardamom, and Rose Water
      Sharbat, 231
    Saffron and Cardamom Milk, 235
    Salted Tarragon Lassi, 232
    Spiced Mango Milkshake, 236
    Toasted Cumin Lemonade, 227

E

Eggplant Pilaf, 102–3
Eggs
    Baked Eggs with Artichoke Hearts, 140
    Bombay Frittata, 137
    Crispy Fried Eggs in Ghee, 255
    Deviled Eggs with Creamy Tahini and
      Za'atar, 144
    Egg Salad with Toasted Coriander, 143
    Hard-Boiled Eggs, 255
    shopping for, 136
    Toasted Naan and Chicken Soup, 76–77
Elderflower, 29
    Elderflower and Ghee Cake, 215
    Watermelon-Elderflower Granita, 195

F

Fats, 86–87, 268–70
Fennel, 27
    Charred Snap Peas and Fennel with Bacon-
      Guajillo Salt, 106
    Cherry-Fennel Barbecue Sauce, 152
    Fennel and Ginger–Spiced Sweet Granola,
      91–93
    Pickled Carrot with Fennel, 273
    Upside-Down Orange and Fennel Cornmeal
      Cake, 216–18
Fenugreek seed, 27
Figs
    Caramelized Fig and Bourbon Iced Chai, 247
    Fennel and Ginger–Spiced Sweet Granola,
      91–93
Fish
    Coriander Gravlax, 133
    Smoked Sardines and Kumquat Crostini, 47
    Tandoori Swordfish Steaks, 127–29
    Turmeric-and-Chile-Roasted Red Snapper
      with Melon Salsa, 130–31
Frittata, Bombay, 137

G

Garam Masala, 263
Garlic, 29, 259
    Charred Green Garlic and Yuzu Ponzu
      Sauce, 277
    Fingerlings with Crispy Sage and Garlicky
      Kefir Crème Fraîche, 110

    Garlic Naan, 95
    Ginger-Garlic Stir-Fried Crab, 124–26
    green, 29
    Pumpkin Garlic Puree, 127–29
    Roasted Garlic, 259
    Roasted Garlic in Sesame Oil, 259
Ghee, 260
Ginger, 29
    Fennel and Ginger–Spiced Sweet Granola,
      91–93
    Ginger and Tamarind Refresher, 228
    Ginger-Garlic Stir-Fried Crab, 124–26
    Ginger-Lemon Relish, 274
    Ginger-Lentil Millet Bowl, 100
    Pineapple Serrano Gin, 243
    Rum-Soaked Raisin Caramel Cake, 220–21
    Spicy Chocolate Chip–Hazelnut Cookies, 203
Granita, Watermelon Elderflower, 195
Granola
    Fennel and Ginger–Spiced Sweet Granola,
      91–93
    Savory Granola, 93
Grape Leaf–Wrapped Shrimp, Grilled, 120–21
Gravlax, Coriander, 133
Grinding, 158

H

Hand Pies, Turkey-Mushroom, 155–56
Hazelnut Cookies, Spicy Chocolate Chip–, 203
Herbs. See also individual herbs
    bruising, 158
    dried, 86
    fresh, 86
    grinding, 158
    infusing, 161
    muddling, 161
    storing, 82
Himalayan pink salt, 25

I

Ice Cream, Jaggery, 199
Infusing, 161

J

Jaggery, 25, 85–86, 152, 199, 253
    Jaggery Ice Cream, 199
Jam, Blackberry Long Pepper, 281
Juniper berries, 27

K

Kala namak, 25
Kale
    Hot Green Chutney, 277
Kebabs, Spiced Beef, 52
Kefir Crème Fraîche, 260
Kosher salt, 25

Kumquats
    Smoked Sardines and Kumquat Crostini, 47
    Turkey Leg Roast with Mixed Citrus and
      Juniper, 151

L

Lamb
    Bone and Lentil Broth, 80–81
    Ground Lamb and Potato "Chops" with
      Sambal Oelek, 175–76
    Lamb Chops with Red Lentils, 178–80
    Roast Leg of Lamb, 181–83
Lassi, Salted Tarragon, 232
Lemons
    Ginger-Lemon Relish, 274
    Lemon Simple Syrup, 225
    Orange Blossom Lemonade, 225
    Spiced Lemon Pickle, 274
    Toasted Cumin Lemonade, 227
Lentils
    Bone and Lentil Broth, 80–81
    Cocoa-Spiced Bean and Lentil Soup, 73
    Ginger-Lentil Millet Bowl, 100
    Lamb Chops with Red Lentils, 178–80
    Roasted Cauliflower, Paneer, and Mixed
      Lentil Salad, 64
Limes, 85
    Chicken Noodle Soup with Omani Limes, 79
    Chouriço Potato Salad, 69
    Curry and Makrut Lime Leaf Salt, 267
    leaves, makrut, 29
    Omani, 25
    Toasted Cumin and Lime Cucumber Salad,
      59
    Turmeric and Lime Mussel Broth, 116
Long pepper, 23
    Blackberry Long Pepper Jam, 281

M

Mace, 27
Mangoes
    Crab Cakes with Lemongrass and Green
      Mango, 123
    green, 25
    Green Mango Tartar Sauce, 281
    Spiced Mango Milkshake, 236
Maple syrup, 25
    Spiced Maple–Broiled Peaches, 200–201
    Spiced Maple-Vinegar Syrup, 200
Margherita Naan Pizza, 99
Marinating, 161, 163
Masala Chai, 264
Meat Loaf, Spiced, 167–69
Milkshake, Spiced Mango, 236
Millet Bowl, Ginger-Lentil, 100
Mint, 29
Moscow Mule, Pomegranate, 244

Mostarda, Apple and Pear, 281
Muddling, 161
Mushrooms
    Butternut Squash and Tea Soup, 70
    Turkey-Mushroom Hand Pies, 155–56
Mussel Broth, Turmeric and Lime, 116
Mustard seed, 27

N

Naan, 94–95
    Garlic Naan, 95
    Margherita Naan Pizza, 99
    Toasted Naan and Chicken Soup, 76–77
Nigella seed, 27
Nit'r Qibe, My, 270
Noodle Soup, Chicken, with Omani Limes, 79
Nori, 29
    Nori and Yuzu Ponzu Salt, 267
Nutmeg, 27
Nuts. *See also individual nuts*
    Chile-Sumac-Pomegranate Nuts, 37
    soaking in water, 235

O

Oats
    Fennel and Ginger–Spiced Sweet Granola,
      91–93
    Savory Granola, 93
Oils, 86–87
Okra, Chickpea-Battered Fried, 38
Olives, Chipotle–Garam Masala, 34
Omani limes, 25
    Chicken Noodle Soup with Omani Limes, 79
Onions, Red, with Coriander, 274
Orange blossom water, 29
    Orange Blossom Lemonade, 225
Oranges
    Steak with Orange Peel and Coriander, 173
    Turkey Leg Roast with Mixed Citrus and
      Juniper, 151
    Upside-Down Orange and Fennel Cornmeal
      Cake, 216–18
Oysters
    Broiled Herbed Oysters, 42–43
    Oysters with Passion Fruit Mignonette, 115

P

Paneer, 260
    Chouriço Potato Salad, 69
    Roasted Cauliflower, Paneer, and Mixed
      Lentil Salad, 64
Paprika, 23
Passion Fruit Mignonette, Oysters with, 115
Peaches
    Bellini with Cardamom and Peppercorns,
      240
    Spiced Maple–Broiled Peaches, 200–201

Pear Mostarda, Apple and, 281
Peas
    Charred Snap Peas and Fennel with Bacon-
      Guajillo Salt, 106
    Eggplant Pilaf, 102–3
Pickles
    Pickled Carrot with Fennel, 273
    Pickled Green Tomatoes with Mixed
      Peppercorns, 273
    Red Onions with Coriander, 274
    Spiced Lemon Pickle, 274
Pilafs
    Eggplant Pilaf, 102–3
    Simple Pilaf, 256
Pineapple
    Pineapple Serrano Gin, 243
    Rum-Soaked Raisin Caramel Cake, 220–21
Pistachios
    Chile-Sumac-Pomegranate Nuts, 37
    Roast Leg of Lamb, 181–83
Pizza, Margherita Naan, 99
Pomegranate
    Chile-Sumac-Pomegranate Nuts, 37
    molasses, 25
    Pomegranate Moscow Mule, 244
Poppy seeds, 27
Pork
    Chaat Masala–Grilled Pork Chops, 184–85
    Crispy Pork Belly Bites, 54–55
    Homemade Goan-Style Chouriço, 191
    Pulled Pork Tacos with Apple and Serrano
      Slaw, 186–87
Potatoes
    Chouriço Potato Salad, 69
    Fingerlings with Crispy Sage and Garlicky
      Kefir Crème Fraîche, 110
    Ground Lamb and Potato "Chops" with
      Sambal Oelek, 175–76
Puff pastry
    Turkey-Mushroom Hand Pies, 155–56
Pumpkin Garlic Purée, 127–29

R

Rainbow peppercorns, 23
Rainbow Root Raita, 63
Raisins
    Fennel and Ginger–Spiced Sweet Granola,
      91–93
    Grilled Dates and Raisins with Black Pepper
      and Honey, 33
    Rum-Soaked Raisin Caramel Cake, 220–21
Raita, Rainbow Root, 63
Raspberry-Shiso Sorbet, 196
Red Snapper, Turmeric-and-Chile-Roasted,
    with Melon Salsa, 130–31
Relish, Ginger-Lemon, 274